Tick...Tick...

Hear that clock ticking? It's the countdown to the AP U.S. Government and Politics Exam, and it'll be here before you know it. Whether you have one year or one day to go, now's the time to start maximizing your score.

The Test Is Just a Few Months Away!

The rest of us are jealous—you're ahead of the game. But you still need to make the most of your time. Start on page 196, where we'll help you **get the most out of class** and manage the stress of a heavy workload. Plus, we have plenty of material for you to review as you study in class.

Actually, I Only Have a Few Weeks!

That's plenty of time for a full review. Start with the **Comprehensive Review** on page 39. Then learn how to beat the test using our full arsenal of **Multiple-Choice and Free-Response Strategies** (pages 43, 51).

Let's Be Honest. The Test Is Tomorrow and I'm Freaking Out!

No problem. Read through the **Big Ideas of AP U.S. Government and Politics** (page 5). Then get a quick tutorial on how to maximize your score with our tried and tested **Test-Taking Tips** (page 31). If you have time, take a practice test (page 187). Before you go to bed, go through the **Checklist for the Night Before** (page 3) and keep it close. It'll walk you through the next twenty-four hours.

Relax. Everything you need to know, you've already learned. We're just here to keep it fresh in your mind for test day.

My Max Score

AP U.S. GOVERNMENT & POLITICS

My Max Score

AP U.S. GOVERNMENT & POLITICS

Maximize Your Score in Less Time

Del Franz

Published by Sourcebooks, Inc.
P.O. Box 4410, Naperville, Illinois 60567-4410
(630) 961-3900
Fax: (630) 961-2168
www.sourcebooks.com

Library of Congress Cataloging-in-Publication Data

Franz, Del.
  My max score AP U.S. government & politics : maximize your score in less time / by
Del Franz.
      p. cm.
  1. United States—Politics and government—Examinations—Study guides. 2. Advanced
placement programs (Education)—Examinations—Study guides. 3. College entrance
achievement tests—United States—Study guides. I. Title. II. Title: AP United States
government and politics. III. Title: Advanced placement United States government and
politics.
  JK276.F74 2011
  320.473076—dc22

                            2010037503

          Printed and bound in the United States of America.
              VP 10 9 8 7 6 5 4 3 2 1

Contents

Introduction   ix

The Essentials: A Last-Minute Study Guide   1

The Big Ideas of AP U.S. Government and Politics   5

Basic Test-Taking Strategies   31

The Main Course: Comprehensive Strategies and Review   39

Mastering the Multiple-Choice Section   43

Mastering the Free-Response Section   51

Key Terms of AP U.S. Government and Politics   55

Topic 1: The Constitution and the Basic Principles
   of American Government   85

Topic 2: Federalism   95

Topic 3: Congress: The Legislative Branch   103

Topic 4: The President and the Executive Branch   115

Topic 5: The Supreme Court and the Federal Judiciary   129

Topic 6: Civil Liberties   137

Topic 7: The Struggle for Equal Rights   147

Topic 8: Political Parties and Elections   155

Topic 9: Interest Groups   167

Topic 10: Political Culture and the Mass Media   175

Topical Review Answers and Explanations   183

The Big Picture: How to Prepare Year-Round   193

AP U.S. Government and Politics Practice Exam   203

About the Author   255

Introduction

Everybody comes to an AP test from a different place. For some, it's the one AP test of their high school career, while for others, it's just one of many. Some students have been focused on it all year, supplementing their classwork with extra practice at home. Other students haven't been able to devote the time they would like—perhaps other classes, extracurricular activities, after-school jobs, or other obligations have gotten in the way. Wherever you're coming from, this book can help. It's divided into three sections: a last-minute study guide to use the week before, a comprehensive review for those with more than a week to prepare, and a long-term study plan for students preparing well in advance.

Think of these sections as a suggestion rather than a rigid prescription. Feel free to pick and choose the pieces from each section that you find most helpful. If you have time, you should review everything—and, of course, take as many practice tests as you can.

Whether you have a day or a year to study, there are a few things you should know before diving in. For starters, what is the AP U.S. Government and Politics Exam?

About the Test

The AP U.S. Government and Politics Exam is a two-part test. Part I, the multiple-choice section, last 45 minutes and is comprised of 60 questions. Part II, the free-response section, lasts 100 minutes and includes four essay questions. Each part is worth 50 percent of your grade

How It Breaks Down

According to the College Board, the materials covered on the AP exam break down as follows:

Subject	Percentage of Questions
Constitutional Underpinnings (the formulation of the Constitution and its basic tenets)	5 to 15 percent
Political Beliefs and Behaviors	10 to 20 percent
Political Parties, Interest Groups, and Mass Media	10 to 20 percent
Institutions of National Government (Congress, the President, the Bureaucracy, and Federal Courts)	35 to 45 percent
Public Policy	5 to 15 percent
Civil Rights and Civil Liberties	5 to 15 percent

How the Test Is Graded

As you probably know, the test is graded on a scale of 1 to 5. Most colleges will offer college credit for a score of 5, somewhat fewer will give credit for a 4, and even fewer for a 3. If you know which college you're planning on attending, it's a good idea to contact them to see what score is required to be awarded credit.

There is no hard and fast rule of what will earn you a 5, but the following chart gives you a general idea of how many multiple-choice questions you will need to answer correctly to earn each score, assuming you did equally well on the essay section.

Score	Multiple-Choice Score	Percentage of Students Who Earned This Score in 2009
5 (Extremely Qualified)	49 to 60	13 percent
4 (Well Qualified)	40 to 48	17 percent
3 (Qualified)	28 to 39	25 percent
2 (Possibly Qualified)	19 to 27	24 percent
1 (Not Recommended)	0 to 18	20 percent

Of course, you'll be among the 30 percent who score a 4 or a 5, right? If you can make sure you understand the key concepts, as well as the best strategies for bringing them out in the test, there's every reason to be confident you will.

Visit mymaxscore.com for an additional practice test for the AP U.S. Government & Politics Exam, as well as practice tests for other AP subjects.

THE ESSENTIALS: A LAST-MINUTE STUDY GUIDE

If you're just opening this book a few days or hours before the test, don't panic—you're not alone. Many AP students, for different reasons, cram the night before for the AP U.S. Government and Politics test. If you've been taking a U.S. Government and Politics class, you have been preparing all year.

The Last-Minute Study Guide takes you through the few final steps to put you in the best position to score well on the test. Carefully and calmly work through these three steps or as many of them as you can. If you've waited until a night or two before the test, focus on your weak points. Whatever you do, read through the test-taking tips, since even a few minutes spent understanding how to most effectively attack the test could lead to a big improvement in your score.

Step One: Review the Big Ideas

Don't bother trying to review everything you learned in class this year. Instead, read through a summary of the Big Ideas of AP U.S. Government and Politics (page 5) to quickly refresh your memory and focus your review on what's going to be really important on the test. Most questions on the test will relate in some way to these big ideas. If there are any of the seventeen ideas that leave you completely lost, spend a little more time on them. Turn to the Comprehensive Review (page 39) and read over the sections that relate to that topic.

Step Two: Follow the Test-Taking Tips

In any last-minute test prep effort, probably even more important that reviewing the content is making sure you're ready for the testing process itself. You need to know how to approach the test, how quickly to work, common mistakes to avoid, and, of course, when you should guess. The strategies you'll need to know are simple and based on common sense. Yet few test takers employ all these strategies to their advantage. Following the chapter on the big ideas, you'll find a chapter on basic test-taking tips (page 31). You'll find strategies for both the multiple-choice and the free-response sections of the test.

Step Three: Take a Practice Test

Even if your time is very limited, you should take a practice test for AP U.S. Government and Politics. Taking a practice test will show you what you're up against so that you won't be surprised on test day. In addition, taking a timed practice test is the only way you can practice pacing yourself so you can use the limited time most effectively. Whenever you take a practice test, try to recreate, as much as possible, actual exam conditions. Time yourself and take the test without interruptions. If you've waited until the last day or two before the test and don't have an hour and forty minutes to practice the free-response section of the test in full, just take a few minutes to read the free-response test questions and practice thinking through and outlining your answers, rather than writing them out. You'll find a practice test at the end of the book (page 203), and there's an additional practice test online.

Step Four: Be Prepared

At this point, the best thing you can do is be physically prepared for the test. Use this checklist to help you plan and get organized so that you don't forget anything on test day.

Checklist for the Night Before

- **Gather the things you'll need the night before the test.** Locate your social security number and, if you are not taking the test at your own school, be sure to have a photo ID as well. Get everything you need together, including the clothes you plan to wear. Doing this will help reduce stress and allow you to sleep better.

- **Bring good writing implements.** You'll need several sharpened #2 pencils for the multiple-choice section and several pens with blue or black ink for the free-response section. Test the erasers on your pencils; if they do not work well or leave smudges, bring a separate eraser.

- **Don't forget a watch.** There may not be a clock in the testing room and you'll need this to pace yourself.

- **Get a good night's sleep.** Try to relax and sleep well. Do a physical workout of some type to burn off nervous energy if you're feeling stressed. If you're having trouble getting to sleep, do something that might make you drowsy like reading, but don't take a medication to help you sleep unless you normally do this.

- **Get up early enough so you're not rushed.** Set an alarm and have a back-up plan in case it doesn't go off (either another alarm or someone to wake you). You don't want to miss the test because you overslept.

- **Eat a healthy breakfast.** If you normally eat a healthy breakfast, go ahead with your usual breakfast on the morning of the test. Don't drastically change your eating habits or your coffee intake. However, if you don't normally eat breakfast at all, you'll need to change this pattern and have a light, but healthy, breakfast so you can stay alert and energized for the three hours you'll be taking the test.

- **Take a healthy snack.** You can't eat during the test, but during the short break between the sections of the test, you might want to have a quick snack. It's probably a good idea to take something healthy with you to munch on at the break.

  Good luck!

The Big Ideas of AP U.S. Government and Politics

T here are some things guaranteed to be on the AP test. You can be certain that there will be multiple-choice questions that relate to each of the following topics. Each of the free-response questions will probably also incorporate at least one of these topics. If you do nothing else to review for the test, make sure you understand these seventeen fundamental concepts. Here are quick summaries of the most important "big ideas" or concepts of AP U.S. Government and Politics:

1. Federalism

Federalism refers to the sharing of power and authority between the federal government and the state governments. The authors of the Constitution intended to establish a stronger national government but still maintain independent state governments. Each generation since has struggled to define the balance of power between state and federal governments.

The traditional view of federalism was **dual federalism**. Under this concept, the federal government had sovereignty (supreme authority) in certain policy areas such as national defense and interstate commerce, while state governments were sovereign in other policy areas such as education and intrastate commerce. The Constitution lists powers of the federal government and reserves powers to the states. This doctrine held it was possible—and desirable—to assign specific policy areas to the federal government and others to state governments.

Today federalism has evolved so that the idea of dual federalism is largely outdated. The federal government has become the leader in policy areas such as education that were at once the exclusive preserve of the states. Today federalism is often defined by the concepts of cooperative federalism and fiscal federalism. **Cooperative federalism** is used to describe how federal and state governments often work together to try to solve national problems such as poverty or underperforming educational systems, with both states and the federal government establishing and administering programs. **Fiscal federalism** describes the growing tendency for the federal government to establish broad national policies and guidelines in all areas of public policy through the regulations accompanying federal grants. Technically, states can refuse federal money (and thus not be subject to the federal regulations), but, in practice, they seldom do. However, although the federal government becomes the dominant policy maker under fiscal federalism, states retain considerable power and are the actual administrators of the programs established by federal grants.

The supremacy of the national government over state governments was firmly established in *McCulloch v. Maryland* (1819). In this landmark case, the Supreme Court interpreted the **"necessary and proper" clause** of Article I of the Constitution to give the federal government broad powers and prohibited states from trying to regulate the programs or counteract the laws of the federal government.

The **interstate-commerce clause** of Article I of the Constitution has also been a basis for the broad powers accorded the federal government. This clause gives control of interstate commerce to the federal government and has allowed it to get involved in almost all areas of public policy. Many of the groundbreaking laws Congress has passed from the Civil Rights Act of 1964 (which desegregated privately owned public accommodations—hotels, restaurants, retail stores, etc.) to the Health

Care Reform Act of 2010 (which regulates health insurance companies) have been based on the broad powers of the federal government to control interstate commerce.

Today, federalism has evolved from the concept of dual sovereignty to a concept in which the federal government has more power and authority than state governments in determining national policy. Yet, state governments remain independent entities and are the primary administrators of government programs affecting the day-to-day life of Americans. State governments also act as program laboratories, trying new policy and program ideas, which, if successful, can be adopted nationally.

2. Separation of Powers

The U.S. Constitution embodies the concept of **separation of powers** by dividing the government into three independent branches, each with its own function. The legislative branch (Congress) makes the law, the executive branch (the president and the federal bureaucracy) carries out or enforces the law, and the judicial branch (the Supreme Court and the federal judicial system) interprets the law and the Constitution.

The separation of powers results in each branch of government being an independent entity deriving its authority directly from the Constitution. No one branch was intended to dominate American government; in fact, the division of government into three equal independent branches was seen by the authors of the Constitution as a way to prevent any one governmental body from gaining too much power and becoming tyrannical.

3. Checks and Balances

A system of **checks and balances** was written into the Constitution to further guarantee that no one branch of government would be able to become too powerful and tyrannical. While each branch performs its own function, it also has the power to act to check or block the other branches of government. A system of checks and balances can exist only in governments with powerful, independent branches of government.

Under the U.S. Constitution, Congress can block the president by changing or creating laws (including overriding a presidential veto, if necessary), refusing to approve treaties, stopping funding for programs or wars, or rejecting presidential nominees to important positions in the federal government. Among the actions the president can take to check Congress are: vetoing legislation, making executive agreements with other nations rather than official treaties, making recess appointments to important federal government positions when Congress is in recess, or simply using the "bully pulpit" (the power of the president to get media attention) to criticize Congress and sway public opinion.

Congress can check the power of the Supreme Court by proposing constitutional amendments or impeaching justices. The president and Congress can check the Supreme Court by passing new legislation that gets around Supreme Court objections, filling vacancies on the Supreme Court with justices more to their liking, or even expanding the number of justices on the Supreme Court and selecting justices more to their liking for the new positions.

The Supreme Court has the power of **judicial review**—the power to declare laws passed by Congress or executive actions of the president and federal agencies unconstitutional. This power is not written into the Constitution but was established by the Supreme Court itself in *Marbury v. Madison* (1803). The Supreme Court functions as the final interpreter of federal law and the Constitution, allowing it to check the power of the president and Congress.

One area of continuing controversy regarding checks and balances is the **War Powers Resolution** (also known as the War Powers Act). The Constitution provided Congress with what was intended as a powerful check on the president's power as commander in chief: the power to decide whether or not to declare war. However, in the modern world, the idea of a declaration of war is largely outdated. The fact that the president can now send troops into combat overseas for an indefinite time period without a declaration of war has eliminated the check Congress once had on such action. As a result, Congress passed the War Powers Act over Nixon's veto in 1973 to create a check on the president's power to conduct undeclared war. This act requires the president to notify Congress if U.S. troops are sent into combat abroad and requires the withdrawal of the troops within 60 days unless Congress declares war or adopts a resolution approving the action. Presidents from Nixon on have not accepted this act, claiming it is an unconstitutional revision of the Constitution. The Supreme Court has not ruled on this issue. Regardless of its uncertain constitutional status, presidents generally seek some resolution from Congress in support of military action abroad and Congress can still check the power of the president by refusing to appropriate money for the military action.

4. The Constitution and Limited Government

Limited government—also known as **constitutionalism**—is the idea that government is limited to the powers granted it by the governed. Usually a written document known as a constitution defines and limits the powers of government and serves as the supreme law of the land. Constitutionalism and limited government are basic principles that form part of American political culture. A country's **political culture** is composed of the core beliefs shared by virtually all the population, regardless of their political leanings or political party affiliations.

The **U.S. Constitution** was written in 1787 by the **Constitutional Convention**, composed of delegates from twelve of the thirteen original states of the United States. It became operational in 1788 after ratification by nine states; it was eventually ratified by all thirteen states. The U.S. Constitution replaced the Articles of Confederation (1777) as the constitution of the United States. The **Articles of Confederation** created a weak national government with only a legislative branch, known as the Continental Congress.

There were many disagreements among the delegates to the Constitutional Convention on how the U.S. government should be structured. As a result, a number of compromises were reached to get the support of a majority of the delegates. The most important of these was the **Great Compromise** (also known as the **Connecticut Compromise**). This compromise ended a dispute between large and small states over representation in the new government. The new Congress was to be **bicameral** with each state getting equal representation in the Senate and each state's representation in the House of Representatives dependent on the state's population. For any law to pass, it must pass both houses of Congress.

Amendments can be added to the U.S. Constitution, but the process is not easy and can usually only be accomplished if a large majority of the American people support the amendment. Congress can propose an amendment by passing it by a two-thirds majority in both houses of Congress. Proposed amendments must be ratified by three-fourths of the states to become part of the Constitution. Unless a limit is stated in the amendment, there is no time limit on the ratification process; an amendment on salaries for members of Congress officially proposed by Congress in 1789 was finally approved by three-fourths of state legislatures in 1992 to become the Twenty-seventh Amendment. A high regard for the original U.S. Constitution is part of American political culture and it has been amended only seventeen times since the Bill of Rights (the first ten amendments) was ratified in 1791.

---

5. Civil Liberties and the Bill of Rights

An important part of the idea of limited government in American political culture is the belief that individuals have rights, also known as **civil liberties**. Many people opposed adoption of the new Constitution believing it did not do enough to protect civil liberties. To get enough support to ratify the Constitution, supporters of ratification (known as **Federalists**) agreed to begin the process of amending the Constitution to add a statement of rights as soon as it was ratified. The first ten amendments to the Constitution, known as the **Bill of Rights**, became part of the Constitution in 1791. The Bill of Rights requires the federal government to respect a wide range of civil liberties, the most important of which are described in greater detail below:

- **First-Amendment freedoms** The rights contained in the First Amendment—freedom of expression and freedom of religion—are of such importance that they will be discussed as separate "big ideas" (see #6 and #7 below).
- **Right to bear arms** The interpretation of the Second Amendment is controversial. Until this decision, the Supreme Court had held that, due to the wording of the amendment, the right to bear arms was connected to service in a state militia. In *District of Columbia v. Heller* (2008), however, the Court reversed itself and declared a constitutional right to gun ownership independent of being a member of a state militia.
- **Protection from unreasonable searches and seizures** The Fourth Amendment establishes the right of the people "to be secure in their persons, houses, paper, and effects against unreasonable searches and seizures." Search warrants, approved by a judge, may only be issued after police describe what they are looking for and show "probable cause" that it's in the place to be searched. Persons can only be stopped when there is probable cause to believe they have committed a crime.
- **Due process of law** This is the concept that government must act in a fair matter in accordance with established laws and procedures. The Fifth Amendment requires due process of law in criminal proceedings and in taking private property for public use (eminent domain).
- **The rights of the accused** The rights of those persons accused of a crime are contained in the Fifth and Sixth Amendments of the Bill of Rights.

These rights include the right to an attorney, the right to confront witnesses against you, the right to remain silent, the right to a speedy trial, and the right to trial by an impartial jury. The Warren Court (1953–1969) extended the rights of the accused. For example, in *Gideon v. Wainright* (1963), the Supreme Court ruled that states had to provide an attorney in felony cases for defendants unable to afford one on their own. In *Miranda v. Arizona* (1966), the Court ruled that defendants not only had the right to have an attorney and to remain silent, but also the right to be informed of these rights when taken into custody.

- **Prohibition of cruel and unusual punishment** The Eighth Amendment prohibits the government's use of "cruel and unusual punishment." However, since what constitutes cruel and unusual punishment is highly subjective, the federal courts have generally allowed Congress and state legislatures to set punishments. Recently, however, the Supreme Court has used the constitutional prohibition of cruel and unusual punishment to overturn state laws applying the death penalty to minors and mentally retarded persons.

- **Right to privacy** Although no individual right to privacy is specifically stated in the Bill of Rights, the Supreme Court has determined that the freedoms in the Bill of Rights imply an underlying right to privacy. The right to privacy was established in *Griswold v. Connecticut* (1965), which declared unconstitutional a state law prohibiting the use of birth control. In *Roe v. Wade* (1973), the Supreme Court determined that the right to privacy is "broad enough to encompass a woman's decision on whether or not to terminate a pregnancy." The Court has also applied the right to privacy to sexual relations between consenting adults; in *Lawrence v. Texas* (2003) it ruled that states could not criminalize consensual sex between adults of the same sex, striking down sodomy laws in the thirteen states that still had them.

- **Fourteenth Amendment's due process clause** The due process clause of the Fourteenth Amendment (1868) does not add any rights to the Bill of Rights; however, the Supreme Court has used this clause to apply the Bill of Rights to state governments, rather than just to the federal government. In *Gitlow v. New York* (1925), the Court ruled that state governments could not restrict the rights of freedom of speech and the press contained in the First Amendment. Subsequent decisions have added most other civil liberties in the Bill of Rights to those rights that state governments must also respect. As a result of the decision in *Gitlow v. New York*, cases involving the abridgement of civil liberties by state government can now be taken to federal courts for consideration.

---

6. Freedom of Expression

The First Amendment guarantees the rights of freedom of religion and freedom of expression—including freedom of speech, freedom of the press, and the right to peacefully assemble to protest. The amendment is the most important of the Bill of Rights since the right to freedom of expression is the cornerstone of the American political system. Without freedom of expression, all other rights and freedoms—and democracy itself—are endangered.

The Supreme Court has vigorously defended the right to freedom of expression, even when it involves expression of views most people find repugnant. While general support for freedom of expression is part of American political culture, Court decisions defending freedom of expression are often politically unpopular. In one such decision, *Texas v. Johnson* (1989), the Supreme Court ruled that flag burning was a form of **symbolic free speech** protected by the First Amendment, declaring a Texas law banning flag burning to be unconstitutional. In *Brandenberg v. Ohio* (1969), the Court held that the First Amendment protected a speech given at a Ku Klux Klan rally calling for the use of illegal force. In this case the Court established the **"imminent lawless action" test**, saying that unless there was the threat of imminent lawless action, the government could not prohibit speech, even if it advocated taking unlawful action.

However, freedom of expression, like other rights, is not absolute. Free expression can be denied if it endangers the national security, deprives others of their rights, or involves obscenity. If false information is spoken (slander) or published (libel), the injured party can sue for damages. Obscenity in public spaces is a form of expression that is not protected by the First Amendment and can therefore be prohibited by government. However, the difficulty in defining obscenity and the danger that government censorship might dampen the flow of information and ideas has led to many obscenity laws being overturned by the Supreme Court.

---

7. Freedom of Religion

The First Amendment guarantees freedom of religion in addition to freedom of expression. It states: "Congress shall make no law respecting an establishment of religion, or prohibiting the free exercise thereof..." These two clauses of the amendment relating to freedom of religion are called the **establishment clause** and the **free-exercise clause**. Although the amendment clearly refers only to Congress and does not include state governments, the language is now also binding on state and local governments as a result of Supreme Court decisions interpreting the due process clause of the Fourteenth Amendment (see "Civil Liberties and the Bill of Rights" above).

The **free-exercise clause** of the First Amendment grants people the right to exercise the religion of their choice without government interference. In *Wisconsin v. Yoder* (1972), the Supreme Court ruled that Amish families were exempt from a state law requiring children to attend school until they were sixteen years of age because of long-held religious practices that prioritized work, family, and church over a high school education. However, in other cases, an overriding state interest has been deemed by the Court to be more important than the free exercise of religion. For example, the Supreme Court has ruled that government, with its overriding interest in protecting children, can require medical treatment for children with life-threatening illnesses even when providing such treatment violates the parents' religious beliefs and practices.

The **establishment clause** of the First Amendment has been interpreted by the Supreme Court as creating a "wall of separation between church and state." In *Engel v. Vitale* (1962) the Supreme Court ruled that the recitation of prayers in public schools was a violation of the establishment clause and therefore unconstitutional. In 1963 it declared that Bible-reading in public schools was also a violation of the establishment clause. In 1987 the Supreme Court, determining that creationism was a religious doctrine rather than a scientific theory (*Edwards v. Aguillard*, 1987), declared a Louisiana law requiring the teaching of creationism alongside the teaching of evolution in public schools to be a violation of the First Amendment's establishment clause. Similarly the Court has banned religious displays (such as nativity scenes, but not Christmas trees) in government buildings or parks.

However, the Supreme Court has taken a pragmatic view, recognizing that governmental and religious institutions often share common goals and may indirectly work together. Thus, the Court has banned state and local governments from paying part of the salaries of teachers at church-affiliated schools but it has ruled that these governments can purchase secular textbooks for these schools. The standard the Supreme Court has applied is called the **"excessive entanglement with religion" test**—if the activity "excessively entangles government with religion," it is unconstitutional. As a result, in 2002 the Court upheld an Ohio law that provided government-funded school vouchers that could be used at parochial schools as well as public schools (*Zelman v. Simmons-Harris*, 2002). Since the program provided vouchers to individuals (rather than parochial schools) and parents had a choice of which school their children would attend, the Court held that the vouchers did not involve excessive government "entanglement with religion."

8. Equal Rights

Although the principle of equality before the law of all individuals goes back to the founding of our nation, in reality, minority groups have often had to struggle to gain equal rights. The most dramatic struggle for equal rights has been that of African Americans; this struggle, especially during the mid-twentieth century, was known as **Civil Rights Movement**.

During the Civil War, Lincoln used his power as commander in chief to issue an executive order, the **Emancipation Proclamation** (1863), freeing slaves in states in rebellion against the United States, but this excluded slaves in five border states that remained in the union and slaves in most areas of the South controlled by the Union army. Slavery did not end until the ratification of the **Thirteenth Amendment** in 1965. With the North's victory in the Civil War, the **Fourteenth Amendment** (1868) was passed, which required state governments to provide "equal protection of the law" to all citizens as well as the **Fifteenth Amendment** (1870), which prohibited states from denying the right to vote based on "race, color, or previous condition of servitude." However, a few years after the Civil War, the Union occupation of the South ended, southern states were readmitted to the Union, and progress towards equal rights for African Americans ended. States passed discriminatory "Jim Crow laws" that segregated the races and kept African Americans from effectively exercising their rights, including the right to vote.

In the 1950s and '60s, the Civil Rights Movement arose. It largely accomplished the object of equality before the law—although not equality of result—for African Americans through a series of changes involving Supreme Court decisions, new laws, executive orders, and an amendment to the Constitution. The chart below summarizes the most important of these:

LANDMARK CIVIL RIGHTS ACHIEVEMENTS

Description	Year	Type of Action	Significance
Integration of armed forces	1948	executive order	Ended racial segregation in the U.S. armed forces
Brown v. Board of Education	1954	Supreme Court decision	Declared forced segregation of races in public schools to be a violation of the equal protection clause of the Fourteenth Amendment. This decision overturned *Plessy v. Ferguson* (1896), which allowed separate facilities for black and white races.
Integration of Central High School, Little Rock	1957	executive order	To enforce ruling in *Brown v. Board of Education*, President Eisenhower ordered federal troops to Little Rock to allow fifteen African Americans to enter Central High School. The Arkansas governor had used the Arkansas National Guard to block them from entering.
Civil Rights Act of 1964	1964	federal law	Congress used its power to control interstate commerce to ban segregation in privately owned public accommodations (hotels, restaurants, stores).
Twenty-fourth Amendment	1964	constitutional amendment	Ended the poll tax, which had been used to discourage African American (and poor whites) from voting.
Voting Rights Act of 1965	1965	federal law	Outlawed discriminatory voting practices, including literacy tests, that had been used to disenfranchise (take away voting rights from) African Americans. States with histories of discriminatory practices were to be monitored by the federal government to make sure they didn't continue to use discriminatory voting practices.

| Loving v. Virginia | 1967 | Supreme Court decision | Overturned a Virginia law that prohibited interracial marriage on the grounds that this violated the equal protection clause of the Fourteenth Amendment. Previously in *Alabama v. Pace* (1883), the Court had found that laws against interracial sex and marriage did not violate the equal protection clause as long as both white and black partners were punished equally. |

Other groups, too, have struggled to achieve equal rights. The **Women's Suffrage Movement** was successful in 1920 when the **Nineteenth Amendment** was ratified giving women the right to vote. However, an amendment proposed by Congress in 1972 to give equal rights to women was approved by only thirty-five of the thirty-eight states required for ratification. Federal legislation, however, including the Equal Pay Act (1970) and the Civil Rights Act of 1964 (see above), has made discrimination on the basis of sex illegal. The Supreme Court ruled in *Reed v. Reed* (1971) that state laws that granted preferences based on gender were unconstitutional.

---

9. The Legislative Process: Laws Pass Only if Supported by a Large Majority

---

Congress dominates the legislative process. The Constitution gives it the power to create new laws (or repeal existing laws), subject only to the check of the president's **veto**. Even if the president vetoes legislation passed by Congress, Congress can **override** the veto by voting on the legislation again and passing it by a two-thirds majority in both houses of Congress.

However, it is very difficult for a **bill** (proposed legislation) to get through Congress to become law. Congress has intentionally created rules that place many hurdles that must be crossed and, to pass some of these hurdles, more than a simple majority is needed. For example, to end debate and vote on a bill in the Senate, three-fifths of the senators must vote in favor of **cloture**. That means that a minority of senators can keep a bill from passing simply by keeping the debate open; this is called a **filibuster**. The result is that, in practice, getting a bill through Congress requires a considerable majority (sometimes referred to as a "supermajority") of senators and representatives in support of the bill. This guarantees that laws that pass have broad support; however, it also means that the legislative process is slow and often deadlocked with neither side having enough support to pass new legislation.

Both houses of Congress operate under similar systems in which **standing committees** hold most of the power. Each committee has its own area of jurisdiction (for example, banking, agriculture, commerce). Leadership in Congress is fragmented, even when the same party controls both houses of Congress. No official can speak for Congress and, within each house, leadership is divided among committee chairs and leaders of the majority and minority parties. This fragmented leadership structure means it is difficult for Congress to act quickly and decisively; instead the legislative process slowly inches forward as consensus is built and compromises are forged.

The process a bill must go through to pass is similar in each house of Congress. Any member of Congress can introduce a bill, which is then referred to the committee whose area of jurisdiction includes the subject matter of the bill. Most bills die at this point; the committee selects a few bills for consideration, which is usually first done by a subcommittee. If a bill is to pass it must gain the support of the subcommittee, then gain the support of the full committee, then pass hurdles to make it to the floor of the House or Senate for debate, then get through the cloture process (which in the Senate is difficult due to the filibuster possibility), and finally be voted on and perhaps pass. If it passes, it must go through the whole process again in the other house of Congress. Even if a bill passes both houses of Congress, it seldom passes with exactly the same language. In that case, a **conference committee**, consisting of members of both the House and the Senate, is appointed to work out compromise language that can gain the support of both houses. If the same bill passes both houses, it goes to the president for his signature or veto.

---

10. The President as National Leader

The Constitution envisioned a federal government led by Congress. Until the twentieth century, the president was usually seen as an administrator carrying out the laws passed by Congress. The actual powers given the president by the Constitution were modest. He is commander in chief of the armed forces, chief executive officer of the federal bureaucracy, and chief diplomat. During most of the nineteenth century, when the armed forces, the federal bureaucracy, and the U.S. role in world affairs were all small, the president's power was also small. The explosive growth of the **federal bureaucracy**, the armed forces, and the U.S. role in world affairs during the twentieth century are factors that helped change the role of the president to one of national leader.

In part, the president has assumed the role of national leadership by default. Congress, with its fragmented leadership and inability to take quick, decisive action, simply can't compete. The president is the only nationally elected leader and, as such, accountable to the American people as a whole, rather than just the people of a particular state or congressional district.

Theodore Roosevelt, president from 1901–1909, defined the role of the modern presidency as an assertive, independent, national leader. Roosevelt defined the **activist presidency**, declaring that, as national leader elected by the people, he was permitted to "do anything that the needs of the nation demanded unless such action was prohibited by the Constitution or by laws." In addition, Theodore Roosevelt was among the first to recognize the power of the president's "**bully pulpit**."

The president gets more media coverage than all members of Congress combined. As a result, he can get the public's attention and influence its views—a power not mentioned in the Constitution but which, in reality, gives the president considerable political clout.

Theodore Roosevelt's view of a powerful, activist presidency was adopted by Franklin Roosevelt and by all presidents since FDR. Today, the public expects the president to be a strong national leader capable of quick and decisive action. As the national leader, he is largely held accountable for how the nation—including its economy—fares. The executive branch is now by far the largest branch of government and, in most analyses, the most powerful.

11. The Federal Bureaucracy: Powerful but Unwieldy

The **federal bureaucracy** consists of all U.S. government agencies (called offices, bureaus, departments, administrations, commissions, as well as agencies). These agencies and their workers operate the U.S. government. The federal bureaucracy administers the national parks, pays social security benefits, controls air traffic, builds dikes to control floods, builds interstate highways, runs veterans hospitals, prints money, delivers mail, gets supplies to troops, controls immigration, provides disaster aid, conducts espionage, monitors the safety of food and drugs, explores space, combats epidemics, collects taxes, and much more. Modern government would not be possible without a large bureaucracy.

The federal bureaucracy's 2.5 million workers are organized and controlled via a system of hierarchical control, formal rules, and job specialization. The president serves as CEO of the bureaucracy, but in reality, his control of the bureaucracy is limited. The president appoints top federal officials, who must be approved by Congress. However, most government employees are part of the **civil service system**, which governs hiring, firing, and promotions on the basis of merit, rather than politics. Although federal agencies are subject to oversight by the president, Congress, and the judiciary, the reality is that federal agencies exercise considerable power in their own right.

Most of the federal bureaucracy is organized into **departments** (for example, Department of Defense, Department of State, etc.). Each department is headed by a secretary who is a member of the president's cabinet. The **cabinet** advises the president but has no power of its own. A few agencies (such as the CIA and Environmental Protection Agency) are not part of the departmental structure and report directly to the president. The Executive Office of the president (EOP) serves the president and its powerful Office of Management and Budget (OMB) helps the president manage the sprawling federal bureaucracy. The federal bureaucracy also includes **independent regulatory agencies**, such as the Federal Reserve (which regulates banks and influences interest rates), that perform regulatory functions and are not subject to direct presidential (or congressional) control.

When Congress passes a law, the appropriate federal agency writes the regulations to carry out or enforce it. Federal regulations constitute **administrative law** and have the full force of law, provided they are based on a reasonable interpretation of the **statutory law** (the law written by Congress). **Federal regulations** are written following a well-defined rule-making process that involving input from the public (primarily involves interest groups affected by the regulations). The president can, but seldom does, get directly involved in the rule-making process. The Office of Budget and Management in the Executive Office of the president must approve major new regulations. The only checks on the rule-making power of federal agencies—outside the executive branch—are Congress's ability to overturn a regulation by passing a new law and the Supreme Court's power to declare a federal regulation unconstitutional. The ability to write federal regulations gives the federal bureaucracy considerable power over the way in which broad national policies are carried out in the real world.

12. The Federal Budget: Setting National Priorities

The federal budget defines the programs and priorities of the U.S. government. Each year a new budget must be proposed by the president and money appropriated by Congress to operate the government and its programs.

The Office of Budget and Management in the Executive Office of the president creates the proposed budget based on budget requests from federal agencies and the instructions of the president. The budget proposal goes to Congress, where Budget Committees in the House and Senate review the overall budget and set spending limits. Then Appropriations Committees in the House and Senate create **appropriations bills** to provide specific levels of funding to federal programs and agencies. After the Appropriations Committee approves an appropriations bill, it goes to the full House or Senate for consideration. Then, like all other bills, after both houses of Congress have passed exactly the same version of an appropriations bill, it goes to the president, who can sign or veto it.

Control of the **appropriations process** gives Congress considerable power over national policies and priorities. Federal programs and agencies need money appropriated by Congress in order to operate. The executive branch is required to spend money on programs and agencies as Congress has directed. Often appropriations bills include **earmarks**— money designated for specific projects that the executive branch is obligated to spend. Members of Congress often use earmarks to bring federal funds to their districts.

Mandatory spending accounts for more than half of the total amount the federal government spends. Mandatory spending includes the amounts spent to fund **entitlement programs**—programs that by law entitle individuals who meet specified eligibility requirements to receive benefits. Entitlement programs include Social Security, Medicare, and veterans benefits. Interest on the national debt is also compulsory spending and comprises about 5 percent of total federal spending. **Discretionary spending** is what is left after mandatory spending on entitlement programs and interest on the national debt are removed. Discretionary spending comprises about 40 percent of total federal spending, more than half of which is spending for national defense.

---

13. An Independent Judiciary

The Constitution established the Supreme Court, which heads the judicial branch—one of three independent branches of the U.S. government. The judicial branch also includes lower federal courts established by Congress. Federal judges at all levels of the federal judicial system are nominated by the president and confirmed by a majority of the Senate. They are appointed to life terms, a fact that makes them, at least to some extent, independent of political pressures since they don't need to worry about reelection. Congress can impeach federal judges, but this has rarely been done.

U.S. District Courts form the lowest level of the federal judiciary. They are courts of **original jurisdiction**, or trial courts. They are the only courts in the federal system where two sides present their case to a jury for a verdict. U.S. Courts of Appeals, the next level in the federal court system, have only **appellate jurisdiction**, meaning that they can only hear cases that have already been tried, but the losing party is appealing the decision. Appellate courts do not hold new trials, but examine the record of the original trial to see if proper procedures were followed and whether the applicable law and/or precedents were correctly interpreted. The Supreme Court is the final level of appeal in the federal court system and its role is to resolve substantive legal issues. If an appellate court decides there are grounds to reconsider a case, it issues a **writ of certiorari** to the lower court asking it to turn over the records of the case. Each year thousands of parties petition the Supreme Court for certiorari, but the Supreme Court grants certiorari to only about a hundred cases. For the Supreme Court to grant certiorari, four of the nine justices must vote in favor. If an appellate court decides not to hear a case, the decision of the lower court stands. The Supreme Court mainly serves as an appellate court, but in cases of lawsuits between states (or involving a foreign nation), it serves as a court of original jurisdiction.

Federal courts can only hear cases involving federal law, treaties, or the U.S. Constitution. State courts hear cases involving state law and state constitutions. In state criminal cases, a defendant who has exhausted all appeals at the state level can file a **writ of habeas corpus** in federal court if the defendant believes the state courts violated his or her constitutional rights. If the federal court decides to grant certiorari, the case can then move into federal court.

The **doctrine of judicial restraint** holds that judges should not decide cases based on their own opinions but instead abide by precedent and defer to elected leaders to make national policies. The **doctrine of judicial activism** holds that the courts should not be subservient to the other branches of government and should take action when the elected leaders have failed to uphold the Constitution. The Warren Court (1953–1969) is often given as an example of judicial activism. Its decision in *Brown v. Board of Education* is an example of judicial activism in that it overturned precedent and established new national policy while elected officials ignored the problem of racial discrimination. Later Court decisions on school desegregation that required school busing to obtain racial balance in schools went even further into the realm of judicial activism.

14. Majority Rule and Elections

The American political system is a **representative democracy**; individuals are elected by the people to represent them in Congress. Federal elections every two years select members of Congress, while presidential elections are held every four years. Federal elections in which there is no presidential election are called **midterm elections**. Voter turnout for midterm elections is generally much lower than for years in which there is a presidential election.

Each state makes its own election laws and conducts its own elections, even for federal offices. Thus, in each state the procedures for becoming a candidate, registering to vote, and even voting are different. For example, in some states you can register to vote on the day of the election; in others you must register by a specified date in advance of the election. In some states voters have the option of voting by mail; in others voter must go to a polling place to vote.

Primary elections select party candidates and general elections select the winning candidate. Some states have **closed primaries**—you can only vote on the ballot of the party with which you are registered. Other states have **open primaries**, allowing voters to select which party's ballot they want to vote on. Washington State and California now use a **nonpartisan blanket primary**—one primary election ballot contains all candidates; voters select one candidate for each office with the top two candidates, whatever their party (or lack of one), winning the primary and going on to run in the general election.

The high cost of mass media advertising means that winning an election takes money—usually a lot of it. A winning candidate in a competitive election for the House of Representatives typically spends a million dollars and, in the Senate, winning candidates often spend upwards from six million and much more in a populous state. Today winning candidates are often wealthy and have access to their own fortunes to help them win. Others must spend much of the time raising campaign funds (often from special interest groups that then expect the candidate to support their positions). Besides raising money, election campaigns usually focus on identifying and winning **swing voters** (undecided voters who could "swing" either way) and getting voters expected to be supportive of a candidate to actually vote (**voter turnout**).

15. The Two-Party System

Since the Civil War, two political parties—the Democratic and Republican parties—have dominated elections in the United States. Historically the parties have not been ideologically rigid and have often shifted their positions in different elections and in different states in order to try to gain the majority support needed to win. In fact, the overriding goal of political parties in the United States is to win elections.

The two-party system has become part of our political culture and seldom can other parties (usually called **"third" parties**) compete with the two well-established parties. In the United States, winner-take-all rules mean third parties are shut out of the process in elections for Congress and the president. For example, in 1992, Ross Perot won 19 percent of the popular vote for president but got 0 percent of the vote in the Electoral College. This contrasts with many other democracies in which seats in the legislature are awarded based on the percentage of the vote the party got in the national election and minority parties often play a role in forming a governing coalition.

To win an election in a two-party system, candidates from the left or right of the political spectrum have traditionally moved to the center in an attempt to build a **coalition** that can get the support of a majority of voters; elections become a struggle for independent voters in the center of the political spectrum. However, in the current highly polarized political environment, this is no longer always true. Candidates may decide their best strategy is to stay far to the right or left of center and win by tearing down their opponent through attack ads and by getting a high turnout of their committed supporters, rather than moving to the center and trying to win majority support based on issues.

In the United States, while the two-party system survives, both political parties have long been declining in power. A growing number of people identify themselves as independents (now roughly one-third of voters), rather than members of either the Republican or Democratic

Parties. **Patronage systems** that once rewarded supporters of the winning party by giving them government jobs have been replaced with a civil service system in which government jobs are filled based on objective tests that measure skills. Primary elections have taken the power of selecting candidates from party bosses and given it to the voters.

---

16. Electoral College and the Selection of the President

The president is selected through a long process involving primaries and caucuses, national party conventions, an intense national election campaign, a popular vote, and an electoral vote. It is long and expensive. The process usually begins at least two years before the election when presidential candidates must begin to raise funds. Ten months before the general election, the presidential primaries and caucuses begin state by state. Most states use **presidential preference primaries** to select delegates to the **national party convention**, but some states use **party caucuses** (meetings in each precinct open to party members). National party conventions held in the summer before the November general election choose each party's presidential candidate, who then chooses a vice presidential running mate.

The general election held early in November selects slates of presidential electors in each state; these electors from all states are collectively known as the **Electoral College**—a body that never actually meets. Each state gets the same number of **electors** as it has senators and representatives in Congress, with the District of Columbia getting three electors—the same as the smallest states. The popular vote in each state selects which candidate's slate of electors are chosen. Most states use a **winner-take-all system**; however, Nebraska and Maine select electors by congressional district, allowing their electoral votes to be divided between the two candidates based on which candidate won in each congressional district. If no candidate has a majority in the Electoral College (the vote is tied or a third party candidate has gotten some votes), then the House of Representatives chooses between the top three candidates in a system in which each state has one vote and a majority of states is required to pick a president. Presidential electors cast a separate vote for vice president; if no candidate has a majority, the Senate selects the vice president.

The campaign strategy of presidential candidates is strongly influenced by the Electoral College system. Because of the winner-take-all system, the presidential candidates usually ignore small states. Large states where polls show an overwhelming majority supporting one of the candidates are also ignored. Candidates focus on a few large **swing states** where polls show either candidate could win.

Due to the winner-take-all system of the Electoral College, the vote in the Electoral College seldom reflects the popular vote. For example in 2008, Barack Obama got 53 percent of the popular vote for president nationwide but 68 percent of the electoral vote. Once in a while—most recently in 2000—the winner in the Electoral College is not the same candidate who got the largest share of the popular vote. Among proposals to change the system is to apportion electoral votes on the basis of the winning candidate in each congressional district, rather than the state as a whole. This would align the electoral vote more closely with the popular vote and, some argue, require presidential candidates to focus their campaigns on more states, but still mean it would be possible for a candidate to win the popular vote but lose the election in the Electoral College.

---

17. Interest Groups and Pluralism

Interest groups, also known as "pressure groups" or "special interests," are formed around a political goal shared by their membership. Some examples are the American Association of Retired Persons (AARP), the National Rifle Association (NRA), the Association of Wheat Growers, Greenpeace, American Civil Liberties Union (ACLU), the U.S. Chamber of Commerce, the American Petroleum Institute, and the AFL-CIO.

Unlike political parties, interest groups focus only on issues related to their area of interest and usually back politicians supportive of their cause in both political parties.

Interest groups seek to influence government policy through **lobbying**. Although the term has a negative connotation, lobbying does not usually involve bribery or corruption; it involves working with supportive officials much more than arguing with unsupportive officials to persuade them to change their views. Lobbyists may represent the interests of professional groups such as teachers or oil companies, or interest groups such as the National Rifle Association or the Christian Coalition. Typical lobbying activities include providing information to public officials, providing campaign funding to supportive politicians, getting the group's members to contact Congress (**grass-roots lobbying**), and conducting public relations campaigns to influence public opinion. Interest groups lobby Congress to influence legislation and federal agencies to influence federal regulations. They also try to influence the federal judiciary; for example, an environmental group might initiate a lawsuit against a polluter or against the government for not properly enforcing environmental protection laws.

Group activity to achieve a political goal is an essential part of democracy and the American political system. However, the authors of the Constitution were worried that an interest group could become too powerful. The best way to control the power of an interest group, James Madison argued in the Federalist Papers, was to have other interest groups that could check it. In a large nation, he thought, there was little chance that one interest group could dominate government. Today the concept of **pluralism**—the belief that the political process is the struggle among different interest groups to control public policy—is widely used to describe and explain the workings of the American political system. Pluralists believe that the political struggle between competing self-interest groups— and the compromises that often result—is the best way to produce effective national policies that promote the society's general interest.

Basic Test-Taking Strategies

Your score on the AP U.S. Government and Politics Exam depends chiefly on your knowledge and understanding of the U.S. political system. But that isn't the only factor determining your score; your score will also reflect your ability to test well on standardized exams. You will need to master not only the subject matter but also the mechanics of the test itself.

I. Strategies for the Multiple-Choice Questions

Section I of the exam is comprised of sixty multiple-choice questions. You've probably encountered this kind of standardized test before. Following each question are five answer choices. You have to select the one answer choice that correctly answers the question or completes the statement. The correct answer to the question is right there in front of you—all you have to do is identify which of the five answer choices it is.

You have to work quickly—but still carefully—through this section. There are sixty questions and only forty-five minutes in which to answer them. Knowing how to efficiently and effectively attack multiple-choice questions will help. In short, your score on this section of the test depends not only on how much you know about U.S. government and politics, but also on knowing and being able to use the most effective strategies to approach multiple-choice questions.

Here are basic strategies for the multiple-choice section of the test. Use these to approach the questions in the most effective and productive way so that you can get the score you deserve.

1. **If you don't know an answer, start by eliminating answer choices.** If you don't know an answer, don't give up. The correct answer is right in front of you. Look at the answer choices and see if you can immediately eliminate one or more of the choices as being obviously wrong. Once you're eliminated the wrong answer choices, guess among the ones remaining. The more answer choices you eliminate, the better your chances of getting the correct answer. You may even find that you can eliminate all but one answer choice—which means you've probably just answered the question correctly!

2. **Answer every question even if you have to take a wild guess.** If you are lost on a question and don't know enough about it to even eliminate answer choices, then take a wild guess. The guessing penalty (points deducted for wrong answers) has been eliminated effective with the 2011 AP tests. Make sure you answer each question. If you're running out of time, fill in answer choices at random. There's no penalty for guessing the wrong answer, and you just might guess correctly!

3. **Skip the hard questions and come back to them later.** The questions are organized in random order; you won't come to the easy questions first and get the hard ones at the end. But, since there is a time limit, you don't want to waste time trying to figure out the answers to questions that you're stuck on until you've answered the easy questions. Every question—regardless of how difficult it is—counts the same in the scoring of the exam. That means that you are better off spending time going through the easier questions first, where you are sure to pick up points. So, if you're stumped by a question, skip it and come back to it later. Besides, later on in the test you may

come to a question or answer choice that jogs your memory and helps you identify the answer to the question you skipped. Usually when you come back to a question, it's not as hard as it first seemed.

4. **Be careful on the answer sheet.** There is nothing that can lower you score as much as mistakes in using the answer sheet. Be sure you are marking the answers in the correct row and keep checking it as you go, especially when you skip questions. Also, be sure you have penciled in the answer space completely and have no stray pencil marks in other spaces. The answer you intended to mark may seem obvious to a human eye, but the answers are scored by machines, not humans. Stray pencil marks where you don't mean to make them or insufficiently strong pencil marks where you do mean to make them may cause the machine to read your answer sheet in a way you didn't intend.

5. **Mark up your test booklet.** While the answer sheet needs to be kept clean and free from any stray markings, the test booklet can be marked up as much as you want. Circle questions you skip. Put an asterisk by any questions you answer but want to come back to if you have more time. Underline terms you are unsure of; perhaps a later question will define the term or jog your memory and you can come back to that question. Make whatever markings you want to help work your way through the questions in the most efficient way and easily find the ones you want to come back to.

6. **Pace yourself.** You will need to be extremely focused and work quickly. Try to work through the test at a speed that will at least allow you not only to get through the entire test, but also have time at the end to go back to questions you skipped or want to consider further. Be sure you have a watch so that you can readily check the time. Also be sure you are familiar with the instructions and question types *before* you take the test so that you don't need to waste valuable test time figuring out instructions or questions.

Just how quickly do you need to work? Keep in mind that there are sixty questions and only forty-five minutes for the test. That means that every fifteen minutes you need to work through at least twenty questions in order to get through all of them. Since you'll want time to come back to of them you skipped or that you answered but want to consider further, your pace should be a little faster. Answering fifteen questions every ten minutes will give you five minutes at the end. Answering eighteen questions every ten minutes will give you more than ten minutes at the end to go back to questions you want to spend more time on. Use timed practice tests to determine the pace that works best for you and then practice your pacing.

7. **Use extra time to check your work.** If you have time left over at the end of the test, go back and check your work. This seems obvious, but many test takers, tired by the testing process, don't do it. Make sure that you have marked your answer sheet correctly. Look for other mistakes you may have made. However, you should resist the urge to second-guess too many of your answers because this may lead you to change an already correct answer to a wrong one. First reactions are often correct.

II. Strategies for the Free-Response Questions

Section II of the exam contains four "free-response" or essay questions. While there are only four questions, each question is generally divided into three or four parts that you will need to answer separately. You will have one hundred minutes (one hour and forty minutes) to complete this section. Although you get more time for Section II, both sections comprise exactly half of your final test score.

Keep in mind that to do well on the free-response questions, you'll need not only to know the answers, but also be able to write coherent— and legible—responses. This section of the exam tests not only your knowledge of government, but also your ability to craft a good essay that answers a complex question.

Although they may resemble essay questions you are used to, the AP essay questions are a little different from those you may find on other tests. The AP questions are very specific and more fact-based; you won't be asked an open-ended question in which you state your own opinion and justify it. The scoring is also very specific; for example, you won't get anything extra for providing three reasons if you're only asked for two.

Below are the basic strategies that will help you to do your best on the free-response questions on test day.

1. **Think first, then write.** One of the mistakes test takers make most often is to begin to write immediately, sometimes before they even read the whole question. The AP U.S. Government and Politics questions are long and complex. Carefully read the entire question, including all its parts, and spend a few moments thinking through your answer before you begin to write. This will help produce a coherent response rather than one that misses the point, is difficult to understand, or even contradicts itself. Successful test takers spend at least five minutes thinking, jotting down ideas, planning, and outlining before they even begin to write a response.

2. **Outline your response before writing.** You will need to arrange your thoughts in a logical, coherent way. But you don't need a formal outline—just jot down or list the points you want to include and organize them. Don't write your notes in the answer book—this is only for your final answers—but you can scribble as much as you want in the question booklet. In fact, since the questions are long and complex, mark up the question as you read it as well as making notes regarding your answer. By scribbling down ideas and notes and then organizing your thoughts before you write, you can collect your thoughts so you can write a more complete and coherent answer.

3. **Answer all parts of the question.** Each free-response question is really a series of short essay questions. You need to answer each part of

the question with a separate short essay. Don't forget to label each of these with the correct number and letter. Each question contains so many parts to make it easier for the human graders to award points in a consistent, standardized way. If you don't answer a part of the question, you will lose points, so be sure to check to see that you've responded to each part before moving on to the next question.

4. **Guess, even when you think you don't know the answer.** There is no guessing penalty, so try to answer every part of a question even if you don't know the answer. Take a stab at it—you can't hurt your score and you may get partial credit. For example, a recent AP exam contained a question asking test takers to describe two provisions of the War Powers Resolution that were designed to limit the president's power. Even if you have no idea what was in this law, make an educated guess regarding two things Congress could require that might limit the president's power in conducting war. If you guessed that the act requires the president to consult with Congress before sending troops into combat abroad or if you guessed that the act imposes time limits on the deployment of troops in combat abroad unless Congress approves the action, you will at least get partial credit.

5. **Pace yourself.** Each of the four questions is worth the same amount in your final score, so you don't want to spend all your time on the first question or two and then realize you don't have time for the last questions. Since you have one hundred minutes for the entire free-response section of the test, you should allocate about twenty-five minutes for each question, including thinking and planning time. In fact, it's a good idea to work a little faster than that so that, after you have finished all the questions, you have a little time left to check your work. Answer each question completely, but the questions are very specific; so once you have responded to exactly what was asked, move on to the next question. The person who rambles on and writes the most will probably not be the one getting the highest score.

6. **Write legibly and coherently.** While the AP U.S. Government and Politics Exam is not a test of writing ability, in the final analysis, you need to be able to use the English language and write well enough so that your answers are clear and coherent or you won't get all the points you deserve. Your handwriting will need to be legible; an illegible response gets no points. So even if it slows you down, write clearly enough so that your essays can be read without too much difficulty. Think of the human graders; you won't score well if you leave them frustrated and confused because they can't read your handwriting or understand your sentences.

7. **Check your work.** Try to work fast enough so that you have a little time at the end, after you have answered all four questions, to go back and quickly reread what you wrote. Fix any words that are illegible, check to see that all your sentences make sense, and that you said what you meant to say. Make sure any revisions you make at this point are clear and legible. In fact, as you write your essays, it's a good idea to leave a wide enough margin to give you room for final revisions and corrections.

THE MAIN COURSE: COMPREHENSIVE STRATEGIES AND REVIEW

L et's say you have a few weeks before the big day. There's still time to work through a steady, low-stress review of the key topics and get familiar with the exam and how to approach it. But you'll need a test prep plan that makes the very best use of your limited time. Just follow the steps outlined here, and you'll be ready to earn a max score.

Step One: Review the Big Ideas

Start out with what's really important—an overview of the big ideas of AP U.S. Government and Politics (page 5). Much of the test centers on these 17 concepts. Knowing and understanding these will get you off to a running start and provide a framework for all the content review that you do.

Step Two: Master the Basic Strategies

While understanding the content is important, it's not everything. The quickest way to improve your score is to master the test-taking strategies you'll need for the AP U.S. Government and Politics Exam. You need to know how to approach the test, how quickly to work, common mistakes to avoid, and of course, when you should guess. You find basic strategies for both the multiple-choice section and the free-response sections of the test starting on page 31 right after the big ideas.

Step Three: Take a Practice Test

Taking a practice test will show you what you're up against. Use the big ideas and practice applying the basic strategies and see how well you do. Use the practice test to identify your weakest points and then focus on these areas during your review. Whenever you take a practice test, try to recreate, as much as possible, actual exam conditions. Time yourself and take the test without interruptions. There's a practice test at the end of the book and an additional practice test online at www.mymaxscore. com/aptests.

Step Four: Go for the Advanced Strategies

Now that you've experienced the test, you're ready to look at an analysis of each question type and the strategies to most effectively approach each of these types. Read Mastering the Multiple-Choice Section starting on page 43 and Mastering the Free-Response Section starting on page 51. Master these strategies and you've mastered the test. The result: the best test score you are capable of.

Step Five: Focus on the Terms

Much of the test is really about terms and the concepts they describe so understanding the terms is the key to a good test score. If your time for content review is short, focus on the terms. If you have more time, merge your review of terms with the content review for each of the ten topics. The terms you need to know for the AP U.S. Government and Politics Exam begin on page 55.

Step Six: Complete the Comprehensive Review

Try to spend about an hour each night going through the review materials for AP U.S. Government and Politics in this book. The content review is divided into 10 topics that coincide with the 10 subheads you'll find in key terms. Review terms and content together and focus on the weak areas you identified when taking the practice test. The content review topics begin on page 85.

Step Seven: Keep Practicing

Taking at least one more timed practice test is the only way you can practice pacing yourself so you can learn to use your testing time most effectively. Remember to duplicate actual testing conditions. Practice all the strategies you've learned. If you still have time, visit the website of the College Board and find the essay questions from the last several years of tests. Do as many of those as you can. If you want more practice, the College Board sells an previously administered AP U.S. Government and Politics Exam that you can use to practice with a real test.

Step Eight: Get Ready and Go!

Now you can be confident you're ready to do your best on the test. The night before the test review the Big Ideas one more time and go over the Checklist for Test Day on page 3. Good luck!

Mastering the
Multiple-Choice Section

A ll the questions in Section I of the exam are multiple-choice questions, but there are five different types of multiple-choice questions you'll encounter. You should spend a few minutes now to make sure you understand each question type so you aren't surprised by what you encounter on test day. In addition, you'll need to know how to most effectively attack each type of question.

General strategies on how to approach this section are found on page 31. However, there are also strategies specific to each question type. Use the information in this section not only to understand the different question types but also to learn specific strategies for answering each one.

The Straightforward Question

The straightforward question is a type of multiple-choice question you are probably quite used to. Some of these are phrased as a question such as "In which of the following scenarios would a presidential veto be most likely overridden by Congress?" Often the "question" is not an actual question but a statement that needs to be correctly completed. An example of this is "The Second Amendment to the Constitution has been interpreted by the Supreme Court to…" Here, you need to find the answer choice that best completes the statement.

Strategy

Whether the question is written in the form of an actual question or a statement that needs completion, your strategy is the same.

1. **Make sure you understand what you are being asked.** Reread the question if it's a complexly worded one. Quickly identify in your mind what you are looking for *before* you read the answer choices. All the answer choices may sound pretty good on their own, so it's important to have identified what the question is asking before you spend time reading them.

2. **Read all the answer choices.** More than one of them may all sound good at first glance; make sure you read all to choose the *best* answer. If you pick the first one that sounds good, you may get the wrong answer to a question that you actually know the answer to.

The Negative Question

The negative question has a twist…you are looking for a *wrong* answer to get the question correct. A negative question could read something like this: "Which of the following is NOT a power given Congress in the U.S. Constitution?" Sometimes the negative question is phrased as a statement you need to complete: "States have all the following powers EXCEPT…" In negative questions, the words NOT or EXCEPT will appear like this in capital letters to make sure you don't miss the twist the question has taken.

Strategy

For negative questions, it's even more important to make sure you understand the question and read all the answer choices. In addition:

1. **Stay focused on the fact you are looking for a "wrong" answer.** If it's phrased as a question, four of the answer choices are correct statements; you need to find the one choice that is NOT correct. Remember, if any part of an answer choice is not correct, the whole statement is incorrect.

2. **Check your answer by "plugging it back into" the statement.** If the question stem is phrased in a way that it asks you to complete a statement, take extra care—this can get confusing. Plug the answer you chose back into the statement and reread the whole statement to make sure you have the correct answer and the negative twist hasn't confused you.

The Chart or Graph Question

You can expect that 10 to 15 percent of the multiple-choice questions will involve a chart or graph. Make sure you feel comfortable with your skills in interpreting charts, tables, and graphs. You'll need to be able to understand pie charts, line graphs, bar graphs, and complex tables. If you're confused by these, go back through your textbook, paying special attention to these and seek out this type of presentation of information in newspapers and magazines so you can practice.

Here is an example of the type of chart you're likely to encounter on the test.

FEDERAL GRANTS-IN-AID TO STATE AND LOCAL GOVERNMENTS

| Year | Current Dollars | | Constant (2000) Dollars | |
	Total Grants (in $billions)	Annual per-cent change	Total Grants (in $billions)	Annual per-cent change
2001	318.5	11.4	310.7	8.7
2002	352.9	10.8	338.4	8.9
2003	388.5	10.1	363.3	7.4
2004	407.5	4.9	370.4	2.0
2005	428.0	5.0	373.6	0.9
2006	434.1	1.4	364.0	-2.6
2007	443.8	2.2	361.3	-0.7
2008	461.3	3.9	357.3	-1.1
2009, estimated	567.8	23.1	440.4	23.3

Source: U.S. Office of Management and Budget

There are two types of chart/graph questions often asked. Big picture questions ask about trends. For example, you could be asked about what trends the table above shows in regard to federal grants to state and local governments. Or you could be asked to identify or compare specific information. For example, regarding in the table above, you could be asked whether the federal grants-in-aid increased between 2006 and 2007 after adjusting for inflation. For this exam, you will need to be able to pick out specific pieces of information as well as be able to identify trends from the charts, graphs, and tables included on the test.

Strategy

Since you are working not from information you already know, but from information first being presented to you on the test, these questions take longer. You'll need time to read and interpret the graph or chart in addition to reading the question and answer choices. Here are some things you'll need to do differently for this type of question:

1. **Interpret the graph or chart first.** Before you read the question, look at the chart or graph to get a general understanding of what it is showing. You won't need to remember specifics since you can always refer back to it, but get an idea of the big picture. Reading the question first is likely to be a waste of time since it won't make sense unless you already have some idea of what it is talking about.

2. **If you don't understand the graph or chart, skip the question and try to come back to it later.** If you don't "get" the chart or graph, just move on. These questions don't count any more than the regular questions but they take more time. There is no sense is spending a lot of time reading the question and the answer choices if you don't understand the graph or chart. Try to come back to it later if you have time.

3. **Pay careful attention to the labels.** For example, "in thousands" means you have to add three zeros to every figure; "in billions" means

you have to add nine zeroes to every figure. "Constant dollars" means the actual dollar amounts have been adjusted to take inflation into account. Unless otherwise noted, you can assume dollar amounts shown in a table are "current dollars," meaning they reflect the actual dollars spent at the time with no adjustment made for inflation.

The Multiple-Choice Question within a Multiple-Choice Question

This is probably the most unusual type of question you'll encounter on the AP U.S. Government and Politics Exam. The multiple-choice question within a multiple-choice question generally is no harder than regular questions, but it is more confusing. You can expect three to five questions of this type on the test.

The multiple-choice question within a multiple-choice question is followed by answer choices identified by Roman numerals. One, more than one, or even all of the answer choices may be correct. Following the answer choices identified by Roman numerals are answer choices identified by capital letters. In the capital-letter answer choices are different combinations of Roman numerals. You need to select the one capital-letter answer choice that is correct.

Confused? The example below will help you visualize the multiple-choice question within a multiple-choice question.

Which of the following groups engage in lobbying activities at the federal level?

I.   Senior citizen groups such as AARP

II. State and local governments

III. Business corporations such as Exxon or Citicorp

IV. Professional organizations such as the American Medical Association (AMA) and National Education Association (NEA)

(A) Only I and IV

(B) Only III and IV

(C) Only I, III, and IV

(D) Only II, III, and IV

(E) All of the groups (I, II, III, and IV)

Strategy

Take the time to be careful with these confusing questions.

1. **Read all the Roman-numeral answer choices and circle the Roman numerals of the all the statements that correctly answer the question.** Circling the correct one(s) will save a lot of time and keep you from continually having to reread the roman-numeral answer choices as you work through the capital-letter answer choices. Remember, you can mark up your question booklet as much as you like.

2. **Don't read all the capital-letter answer choices; just find the one that matches the Roman numerals you circled.** Here's the only case where you don't need to read all the answer choices to make sure you've found the best answer. Just find the answer choice that matches the Roman numerals you circled and move on. By the way, the correct answer to the sample question above is answer choice E—all the groups listed lobby at the federal level.

The Political Cartoon Question

You can expect that one of the questions on the AP U.S. Government and Politics Exam will focus on a political cartoon that is provided as part of the question. You need to be able to interpret political cartoons and identify the viewpoint the author is presenting. But the question itself will be a straightforward one for which you will not need any special strategy. (Refer to the strategy for straightforward questions above.)

You will, however, need to be familiar with styles of expression through political cartoons. Practice interpreting political cartoons in newspapers and magazines and look back through your AP U.S. Government and Politics textbook for examples. If you have an AP U.S. History textbook, look through it for cartoons as well. Make sure you can identify the viewpoints being presented by the authors of the cartoons.

Mastering the Free-Response Section

To master the free-response portion of the exam, it is important to have both a general plan of attack for the section and more specific strategies for each question type. You can find a more detailed overall plan on page 34, but the basics are simple: think through and outline your response before writing; be sure to answer all parts of the question; write neatly; take a guess even if you don't know the answer; and check your work when you are done.

You can expect that each of the four free-response questions will have three or four parts. Each part is actually a separate essay question that you're required to answer. Thus, in effect, there will be twelve to sixteen essay questions you will need to respond to. What follows is a specific plan for how to approach each type of essay question.

The Standard Essay Question—but with the Desired Response Quantified

All of the questions on the AP test are standard essay questions, a type with which you are probably quite familiar. Questions on recent AP Government and Politics exams have asked test takers to do the following:

- Describe
- Define
- Explain
- Identify
- Identify and explain
- Define and explain

But there's a twist that makes these standard questions different from the essay questions you are probably used to answering. On the AP test, the questions will be very specific in regard to quantifying the response that is expected from you. Consider the following examples:

1. Describe **one** way that Congress influences fiscal policy and **two** ways the president influences fiscal policy.
2. Define congressional reapportionment and explain **one** reason why it is important to states.
3. Identify and explain **two** reasons voter turnout is considerably lower in midterm elections than presidential elections.

Most free-response questions on the AP U.S. Government and Politics Exam contain numbers. Look for a number that tells specifically how many limits, goals, ways, or reasons the grader will be looking for. If there is no number, you can assume the sought-after number is one. For example, in the second example above, you can assume only one definition of congressional reapportionment is needed to earn the highest possible score.

The purpose of quantifying the expected result is to help standardize the essay scoring process so it's more objective. Thus, in the free-response section of the test, points are scored for very specific things. If you provide the number of ways, reasons, etc., that is specified—and they are correct—you will earn the highest possible score. If you provide fewer than the number specified, you earn a lower score.

Strategy

Make sure your response provides the number of limits, goals, ways, or reasons requested in the question. However, providing additional ones—although they may impress the grader—will not score any more points. Each essay response should provide exactly the number requested.

An important note: You may have taken a standardized test (such as the SAT) where the essay section allows you to write about personal experience or to take a position on an issue and defend it. There are no essay questions like this on the AP U.S. Government and Politics Exam. All the essay questions are very specific and will require you to define concepts or apply and interpret facts, rather than develop and defend your own opinions.

The Your-Choice Essay Question

While you are required to answer all questions—including all parts of questions—some parts of a question will offer you a choice as to what you write about in your response.

> Choose two of the three Supreme Court decisions below and describe how each of the decisions expanded a constitutional right of privacy.
>
> *Giswold v. Connecticut*
>
> *Roe v. Wade*
>
> *Lawrence v. Texas*

In a your-choice essay question, you have to respond to the question but you can choose, from a list provided, what you want to write about.

Strategy

Read the question carefully to make sure you understand what choice is being offered. Make your choice based on what you know best and avoid the topic about which you have the most uncertainty. Don't waste your time by writing about *all* the choices—writing about more than the prescribed number will waste time without adding any points to your score.

The Essay Question with a Table or Graph

The free-response section of the exam usually includes a question that revolves around a table, chart, or graph that is provided at the beginning of the question. For example, you may be given a pie chart showing the composition of federal spending and then be given essay questions regarding the interpretation of the pie chart itself as well as related concepts such as entitlement spending or discretionary spending.

Strategy

Your strategy for this type of question should be similar to the strategy for multiple-choice questions with charts or graphs. Look at the chart first and make sure you have a general understanding of what it is showing, including trends and relationships. The question will not make sense unless you understand the table, graph, or chart. Also pay close attention to labels. If the table or graph shows quantities in dollars, are they constant or current dollars? Are the quantities in thousands, millions, billions, or trillions? Once you've gotten a grasp of what the chart shows, read the question and go from there.

Key Terms of AP U.S. Government and Politics

To get a good score of the AP U.S. Government and Politics Exam, you need to master the terms that are defined and explained in this chapter. Both the multiple-choice questions and the free-response questions will test your knowledge of the terminology associated with American government. A few of these questions will ask you the meaning of a term; others will simply use one of these terms in the question itself, meaning that to understand the question, you'll need to understand the term. Most of the questions on the test contain at least one of the terms included in this chapter either in the question stem or one of the answer choices.

A good grasp of terminology will help you understand the questions, select the best answer for the multiple-choice questions, and communicate effectively in your answers to the free-response questions. In addition, reviewing the terms will help you review the important concepts of AP U.S. Government and Politics since most of the key concepts are associated with key terms.

The terms are arranged is a logical way that works best for review. The topics that tend to be most prominent on the test are discussed first and the topics without much of a presence on the exam are at the end of this chapter. If you are pressed for time, skip those you feel confident you know and focus on the ones you're unsure of. If you have a question about a term after reading the definition and explanation here, refer back to your textbook. Discuss the topic with a friend or with your teacher if you still have questions.

THE CONSTITUTION AND THE BASIC PRINCIPLES
OF AMERICAN GOVERNMENT

Amendment A change to a legal document. A proposed amendment to the U.S. Constitution must gain the support of a two-thirds majority in each house of Congress and then be approved by three-fourths of the states in order to be ratified.

Articles of Confederation The first constitution establishing a national government for the United States. It was in effect from 1777 until 1788. The Articles created a weak central government that consisted of the Continental Congress. There was no separate executive or judicial branch. The Articles of Confederation were replaced by the U.S. Constitution.

Checks and balances The U.S. Constitution not only creates three separate branches of government, but also creates a system in which the actions of one branch can be blocked, to some degree, by the other two branches. For example, the president can check Congress's power to pass laws by vetoing a bill. However, Congress can check the power of the president to veto a bill by overriding a veto by a two-thirds majority in both houses of Congress.

Confederation (also known as a **confederacy**) A loose union of states or countries in which ultimate authority (sovereignty) remains with the state governments, not the union. The Articles of Confederation created a confederation and, in the Civil War, the South formed a confederacy in which most of the power was to reside with state governments.

Constitution The supreme law of the land that defines what powers government will have and how it will operate. The U.S. Constitution was written at the Constitutional Convention in 1787 and ratified in 1788. It is the shortest and oldest of all the national constitutions in effect today.

Constitutional Convention The body of delegates selected by twelve state legislatures (Rhode Island did not participate) that met in Philadelphia in 1787 to revise the Articles of Confederation. Instead of revising the Articles, they created a new document, the U.S. Constitution. Among the most influential of the delegates was James Madison, who wrote much of the document.

Constitutional democracy The current form of government in the United States, characterized by representative democracy and a government limited by a Constitution. Democracy has taken hold gradually with all white males obtaining the right to vote by the Civil War, African Americans in 1870 (Fifteenth Amendment), and women in 1920 (Nineteenth Amendment).

Constitutionalism The idea that there are limits on the power of government and that these limits can be or are defined in a constitution.

Declaration of Independence (1776) This document declared the independence of the United States from Britain. Written by Thomas Jefferson and based on John Locke's ideas, it declares "inalienable rights" among which are "life, liberty, and the pursuit of happiness." It is only a declaration—it did not create a government, does not have the force of law, and did not establish any rights that can be upheld in court.

Democracy A form of government in which the people rule either directly (**direct democracy**) as in a New England town meeting or through their elected representatives (**representative democracy**). The delegates to the Constitutional Convention opposed democracy; they feared "government by the masses" and the "tyranny of the majority." At the time, only white males who owned property could vote in most states.

Executive branch The branch of the government that carries out or enforces the law made by the legislative branch. The U.S. Constitution establishes an executive branch headed by a president who is indirectly elected by the people. The executive branch includes virtually all the departments, agencies, commissions, and other offices of the U.S. government including the armed forces.

Federalist Papers Essays written by the Federalists (chiefly James Madison, Alexander Hamilton, and John Jay) in support of ratification of the proposed U.S. Constitution. The Federalist Papers are considered among the greatest contribution by Americans to political thought.

Great Compromise (also known as the **Connecticut Compromise**) The dispute between large and small states (in terms of population) threatened to end the Constitutional Convention without an agreement. The Great Compromise (proposed by delegates from Connecticut), created a bicameral legislature. In the House of Representatives, states are apportioned representatives based on the population of the state, while in the Senate, each state gets two senators. A bill must pass both houses of Congress to become law.

Judicial branch The branch of the government that interprets the law and settles disputes regarding the law. The U.S. Constitution establishes a judicial branch headed by the Supreme Court. It gives Congress the power to define and establish the lower courts of the judicial branch.

Legislative branch The law-making branch of government. The U.S. Constitution establishes a bicameral Congress as the legislative branch of the U.S. government. It consists of the House of Representatives and the Senate. Each state is allocated two senators; the number of representatives a state gets in the House of Representatives depends on the population of the state.

Limited government A government whose power is limited by a constitution that defines the lawful use of power. A limited government is limited to the powers given it by the people.

Natural rights (also known as **inalienable rights**) The idea, most closely associated with Enlightenment thinker John Locke, that people have rights and that it is government's duty to protect these rights. Locke believed natural rights included life, liberty, and property.

Popular sovereignty Popular sovereignty is the idea developed during the Enlightenment in Europe that the source of government's authority comes from the people, not the divine right of kings. The U.S.

Constitution, which begins with "We, the people..." embodies the idea of popular sovereignty.

Ratification Ratification refers to the official approval of a document required in order for it to take effect. Once the U.S. Constitution was drafted, it had to be ratified by the states. The debate over ratification pitted **Federalists** (who supported the proposed federal government) against **Anti-Federalists** (who believed the federal government would be too powerful). The Constitution was officially ratified in 1788 after nine states approved it; however, the last of the thirteen states, Rhode Island, did not ratify it until 1790.

Republican form of government The form of government created by the U.S. Constitutional Convention involving limited government, a constitution, elected representatives, and no monarch. According to the Constitution the federal government must guarantee that every state also has a republican form of government.

Separation of powers The U.S. Constitution divides the powers of the U.S. government among three separate, independent branches of government: legislative, executive, and judicial. The purpose of dividing power was to prevent any one branch or institution of government from becoming too powerful. The idea is attributed to French Enlightenment thinker Montesquieu.

Social contract The idea developed during the Enlightenment in Europe that government existed because of an implied social contract between the people and the government. In this social contract, the people gave up some of their freedom in return for the government's establishment of law and order. This idea, associated with Enlightenment thinkers Thomas Hobbes and Jean-Jacques Rousseau, was revolutionary because it held that the power of government came from the people, not God (the divine right of kings).

FEDERALISM

Concurrent powers Powers held by both the federal and state governments. For example, both federal and state governments can institute an income tax, build a road, or charter a bank.

Cooperative federalism This term is used to describe how federal and state governments often work together to try to solve national problems like poverty or underperforming educational systems, with both states and the federal government establishing and administering programs.

Devolution The idea that the federal government should give more authority to state and local governments in administering federal programs and grants. The Welfare Reform Act, which gave state and local governments more power over how federal welfare money is spent, is often given as an example of devolution.

Dual federalism Under this traditional concept of federalism, the federal government had sovereignty (supreme authority) in certain policy areas such as national defense and interstate commerce, while state governments were sovereign in other policy areas such as education and intrastate commerce. This doctrine held it was possible and desirable to assign specific policy areas to the federal government and others to state governments. The concept of dual federalism is largely outdated; both cooperative federalism (see above) and fiscal federalism (see below) are more accurate descriptions of how things work today.

Enumerated powers (also known as **delegated powers** or **expressed powers**) The powers the U.S. Constitution (Article I, Section 8) expressly lists and delegates to Congress and the federal government. These include the powers to levy taxes, regulate interstate commerce, provide for the national defense, and make immigration law, among others.

Federalism The sharing of power and authority between the federal government and the state governments. The delegates at the Constitutional Convention intended to establish a stronger national government but still maintain independent state governments. Each generation since has struggled to define the balance of power between state and federal governments.

Fiscal federalism This term describes the growing tendency for the federal government to establish broad national policies and guidelines in all areas of public policy through the regulations accompanying federal grants to state and local governments. Technically, states can refuse federal money (and thus not be subject to the federal regulations connected to that money), but, in practice, they seldom do.

Implied powers The powers of the federal government to take action that are not expressly stated in the Constitution but which are authorized by the "necessary and proper" clause of the Constitution (see below).

Interstate-commerce clause This clause of Article I of the Constitution gives control of interstate commerce to the federal government and, combined with the "necessary and proper" clause, has allowed it to get involved in almost all areas of public policy. Many groundbreaking federal laws, from the Civil Rights Act of 1964 (which desegregated privately owned hotels, restaurants, retail stores, etc.) to the Health Care Reform Act of 2010 (which regulates health insurance companies), have been based on the broad powers of the federal government to control interstate commerce.

"Necessary and proper" clause (also known as the **elastic clause**) Article I, Section 8 of the U.S. Constitution gives Congress the authority to "make all laws which shall be necessary and proper" to carry out the powers that are enumerated in the Constitution. This clause has been interpreted by the Supreme Court to give the federal government broad powers. In *McCulloch v. Maryland* (1819) the Court established a broad interpretation of this clause to declare the federal government's establishment of a national bank to be constitutional, although no such power was specifically expressed in the Constitution.

Reserved powers Powers reserved to the states under the Tenth Amendment to the Constitution. No specific powers are listed in this amendment; it simply states that powers not given to the federal government are reserved for the states.

Supremacy of the federal government Article V of the Constitution establishes the supremacy of the U.S. government over state governments. *McCulloch v. Maryland* (1819) not only established a broad interpretation of the "necessary and proper" clause, but also strengthened the supremacy of the national government by prohibiting state governments from trying to tax or regulate federal programs or counteract federal laws.

Unfunded mandates An unfunded mandate exists when state and local governments, in order to receive federal grants, are required to take certain actions that involve costs (such as making buildings accessible to persons with disabilities), but these costs are not reimbursed by the federal government.

CONGRESS: THE LEGISLATIVE BRANCH

Bicameral Composed of two chambers. The U.S. Congress and most state legislatures are bicameral; only Nebraska has a unicameral state legislature.

Bill Proposed legislation. Bills are introduced by members of Congress; however, bills having to do with taxation can only be introduced by members of the House of Representatives. Bills must be passed by both houses of Congress.

Caucus An organized group of senators or representatives working together for a common purpose. In both the Senate and House of Representatives, the most powerful caucuses are the party caucuses. But there are many other caucuses, including a black caucus, a women's caucus, and even a GLBT caucus. A caucus tries to unify its members behind a bill or program to maximize its political clout.

Cloture A vote of the House or Senate to end debate and vote on a bill.

Conference committee A committee composed of members of the House and Senate to reconcile similar bills passed by the Senate and House. Both houses of Congress seldom pass exactly the same bill. When both houses have passed similar bills, a conference committee is appointed to negotiate a compromise bill that both houses must then approve in order for it to be sent to the president for his signature or veto.

Congressional committee system In both the houses of Congress, standing committees (permanent committees that continue from one session of Congress to the next) hold most of the power in the legislative process. Committees decide which bills to consider, hold congressional hearings, amend bills, and then, if a majority of the committee supports a bill, report it to the Senate or House floor for debate. Committee chairs are all members of the majority party. Each standing committee is assigned an area of jurisdiction; for example, the House Committee on Agriculture has jurisdiction over federal agricultural policy and dominates the legislative process in this area.

Congressional district The geographic area represented by a member of the House of Representatives. The districts are drawn by state governments in the redistricting process.

Constituents The residents of a senator's state or a representative's district. Since the constituents will decide whether or not a senator or representative is reelected, members of Congress pay close attention to their constituents' individual problems and needs relating to the federal government. **Constituent casework** is an important function of congressional staffs.

Earmarks Provisions in an appropriations bill that require government spending on a certain project. Usually they are inserted into bills by senators or representatives who are trying to get pork-barrel projects for their district.

Filibuster A procedure used in the Senate to block a bill that has majority support from being passed. Senate rules require the support of sixty of the one hundred senators to pass a motion to close debate and vote on a bill. If sixty senators do not vote in favor of cloture, floor debate remains open and a vote cannot be taken.

Gerrymandering In the redistricting process, congressional districts are often designed to produce a certain result in an election. Gerrymandering generally involves cobbling together different areas based on which party these areas traditionally support. Sometimes it produces a very strangely shaped district based on politics rather than geography. A district shaped like a salamander in Massachusetts under Governor Gerry in 1812 is the source of the word.

Impeachment Congress has the power to impeach and convict, thereby removing from office the president, Supreme Court justices, as well as other federal officials and judges. The House has the power of impeachment (bringing charges against the official) by majority vote. The Senate tries impeachment cases with a two-thirds majority required to find the official guilty and remove him/her from office.

Incumbent An office holder that has already been elected at least once and is now seeking reelection. In the House and Senate, incumbents have a tremendous advantage and are usually reelected.

Open seat If there is no incumbent running for reelection, the race is referred to as an open seat election. Neither candidate has the advantages of incumbency, so the playing field of the election is more level.

Pork-barrel spending One way for members of Congress to improve their reelection prospects is to channel federal spending to their home district ("bringing home the bacon"). Pork-barrel projects are local projects funded under the federal budget and include the building and repair of highways, federal office buildings, hospitals, dams, and airports.

Reapportionment The reassignment of seats in the House of Representatives to the states after each national census is conducted every ten years. Seats in the House are assigned to states on the basis of population. Currently, the smallest states have only one representative while the largest, California, has over fifty. Don't confuse with redistricting (see below). The reapportionment of seats to states must be determined before redistricting can begin.

Reconciliation The process of creating a compromise between similar bills passed by each house of Congress (see Conference Committee above).

Redistricting The process each state with more than one U.S. representative uses to define its congressional districts. State laws or constitutions govern the process; in most states, the state legislature draws the districts although the governor often has veto power. The Supreme Court in *Baker v. Carr* has determined that these districts must be as nearly equal in population as possible, but where the lines are drawn is largely up to the state.

Rider A section of a bill that does not relate at all to the subject of the bill, such as a rider on abortion that is attached to a defense funding bill.

Riders are attached by Congress to make it difficult for the president to veto the rider. For example, although the president may oppose the rider on abortion that's attached to the defense funding bill, he may let it pass since to veto it, he would have to veto the whole bill on defense funding, which may contain provisions he strongly supports.

Safe seat A seat in Congress that is not considered competitive. It can be safe because there is a popular incumbent running for reelection or because one party has a large registration advantage (or, as often happens, both of these conditions exist).

Seniority system The system traditionally used in Congress to select chairs of the standing committees. Under this system, the senator or representative of the majority party who has served the longest becomes the committee chair. Currently, a modified seniority system is used in which the chair is determined by seniority in most cases but sometimes, usually with the support of party leaders, the committee bypasses the most senior member to select a different committee chair (often the person ranking next in seniority).

Seventeenth Amendment (1913) Provides for the election of Senators by the people of a state rather than the state legislature

Vacant seat A seat in Congress that is empty because the person holding the office has resigned or died between elections. A special election is called to fill vacant seats in the House of Representatives but most states allow state governors to make temporary appointments of senators who serve until the next general election. Do not confuse open seat (see above) and vacant seat: A vacant seat can only occur between regular elections; an open seat refers to a situation in an election.

War Powers Resolution (also known as **War Powers Act**) A law passed by Congress over Nixon's veto (1973) that limits the power of the president to commit U.S. troops to military engagement abroad without congressional approval. Under the Constitution, only Congress has the power to declare war, giving it what was once an effective check on the president's power. Now that wars are seldom officially declared, however, this Constitutional check on the president's power is no longer very meaningful. The War Powers Resolution addresses this by creating a check on the president's power as commander in chief in an undeclared war. This act requires the president to notify Congress if U.S. troops are sent into combat abroad and requires the withdrawal of the troops within sixty days unless Congress declares war or adopts a resolution approving the action. Presidents from Nixon on have not accepted this law, seeing it as unconstitutional. This issue has not come before the Supreme Court. Regardless of the uncertain status of the War Powers Resolution, presidents generally seek some type of resolution from Congress in support of military action abroad and, in the final analysis, Congress can check the president by refusing to appropriate money for the military action.

THE PRESIDENT AND THE EXECUTIVE BRANCH

Administrative law Federal regulations written by the executive branch to enforce or carry out statutory law. Administrative law has the full force of law, provided the regulations are based on a reasonable interpretation of the statutory law they are designed to enforce.

Cabinet An advisory body to the president consisting of all secretaries of departments plus other federal officials and advisers that the president (or Congress by law) has identified. Today, due to its large size, it performs no important role, with the president getting most of his advice from smaller groups of officials and advisors more focused on a particular issue.

Civil service system The system, which includes nearly all government workers, ensures that they are hired, promoted, and fired based on merit (often measured by objective exams), not politics. At the end of the nineteenth century, the civil service system replaced the patronage system (see below) in the federal government.

Departments The federal bureaucracy is divided into large organizations called departments (for example, the Department of Defense, the Department of Homeland Security). Each department is headed by a secretary appointed by the president and confirmed by the Senate.

Only relatively few federal agencies are "independent" and not part of this departmental structure.

Discretionary spending After interest on the national debt and mandatory spending on entitlement programs are taken out, discretionary spending is what is left. This is spending over which Congress has control, but comprises only about 40 percent of the federal budget. More than half of discretionary spending is defense spending.

Entitlement programs Programs that by law entitle individuals who meet specified eligibility requirements to receive benefits. Examples include veterans benefits, social security, and Medicare.

Executive Office of the President (EOP) The government officials and advisers that directly serve the president (rather than a department or federal agency of some type).

Executive order An order issued by the president to the agencies of the U.S. government, based on Article II of the U.S. Constitution, which vests "executive power" in the president. As chief executive officer of the federal bureaucracy, the president can issue executive orders as long as they do not violate federal law or the constitution. Examples of far-reaching executive orders include Harry Truman's 1948 order to desegregate the armed forces and Bill Clinton's 1998 order prohibiting employment discrimination on the basis of sexual orientation in the federal government. Executive orders can be overturned by passage of a law by Congress or by the Supreme Court. For example, in *Youngstown Sheet and Tube Co. v. Sawyer* (1952) the Court ruled that Truman's executive order placing all steel mills temporarily under federal control, during a strike that closed the mills during the Korean War, was unconstitutional.

Executive privilege The immunity the president and his top advisors have from being required to answer questions or divulge information in congressional hearings. Executive privilege protects the privacy of the president's conversations with his advisors. Although not stated in the Constitution, the Supreme Court has held executive privilege to be part of the separation of powers doctrine embodied in the Constitution.

Federal budget The plan for allocating money to federal agencies and programs for a fiscal year (begins October 1). The federal budget request is prepared by the executive branch and submitted by the president to Congress. Congress revises the budget as it sees fit and appropriates money to federal agencies and programs. There is a **budget deficit** when spending exceeds tax revenues and a **budget surplus** if tax revenues exceed spending.

Federal bureaucracy The federal bureaucracy consists of U.S. government offices and agencies. It is part of the executive branch of government and under the control, at least to some degree, of the president. The federal bureaucracy administers the national parks, pays social security benefits, controls air traffic, builds dikes to control floods, builds interstate highways, runs veterans hospitals, prints money, deploys troops, controls immigration, plans defense strategy, provides disaster aid, conducts espionage, monitors the safety of food and drugs, explores space, combats epidemics, collects taxes, among other functions.

Federal regulations After Congress passes a law, the appropriate federal agency writes the regulations to carry out or enforce the law. Federal regulations are written following a well-defined rule-making process that involves input from the public (primarily interest groups affected by the regulations). The president can, but seldom does, get directly involved in the rule-making process; however, the Office of Management and Budget must approve major new regulations. The only checks on the rule-making power of federal agencies—outside the executive branch—are Congress's ability to overturn a regulation by passing a new law and the Supreme Court's power to declare a federal regulation unconstitutional.

Fiscal policy Fiscal policy, controlled by Congress and the president, involves taxation and spending. Increasing government spending (or reducing taxation) stimulates the economy; decreasing government spending (or increasing taxation) contracts the economy to control inflation. Monetary and fiscal policies form a nation's economic policy.

Independent regulatory agency A government organization that is nominally part of the executive branch but, due to its function as a regulatory body, operates independently of the president (and Congress). Examples: Federal Reserve Board, Federal Trade Commission, Federal Elections Commission, Securities and Exchange Commission.

Mandatory spending Spending on entitlement programs. There is little way to reduce mandatory spending short of changing an entitlement program's benefits or eligibility—actions that are usually politically unpopular.

The modern presidency Refers to the current role of the president as a national leader actively attacking the problems of the country and trying to accomplish his own political goals. During most of U.S. history (except in wartime with the president as commander in chief), the presidency was seen more as an administrator whose role was simply carrying out national policy as determined by Congress.

Monetary policy Monetary policy, controlled largely by the Federal Reserve Board, involves controlling the supply of money to influence interest rates. Higher interest rates slow growth but control inflation; lower interest rates encourage economic growth, but also inflation.

Office of Management and Budget (OMB) The largest and most powerful office of the EOP. It creates the federal budget and assists the president in managing the huge, sprawling bureaucracy.

Patronage system Government jobs given out to reward political supporters

Presidential veto The power of the president to block a proposed law passed by Congress. Congress can override a presidential veto by a two-thirds majority in both the Senate and the House. Since it's usually difficult to override a veto, this power allows the president to influence legislation through the threat of veto, even when he doesn't actually veto a bill.

The president's "bully pulpit" A phrase coined by Theodore Roosevelt (the word *bully* at the time meant "splendid" or "wonderful") to describe the president's ability to command the attention of the media and the people, often giving him the power to set the political agenda and influence public opinion. Although this is not a power granted to the president by the Constitution, in reality it is an important source of presidential power.

Statutory law The body of laws written by Congress

Twenty-fifth Amendment (1967) This constitutional amendment provides for the selection of a new vice president if the office becomes vacant between elections. A new vice president is nominated by the president and confirmed by the Senate and the House by majority vote. This process was used to select Gerald Ford as vice president in 1973. This amendment also describes the process by which the vice president becomes acting president if the president is still in office but unable to perform his duties.

Twenty-second Amendment (1951) Limits the president to two terms in office

Vice president The vice president becomes president if the president resigns or dies while in office. However, the vice president has no official role in government other than acting as president of the Senate—a position that has no power other than breaking tie votes. Since the election of Jimmy Carter in 1976, vice presidents have been assigned important advisory roles by the president.

THE SUPREME COURT AND FEDERAL JUDICIARY

Amicus curiae briefs A brief submitted, not by one of the parties in the case, but by a "friend of the court," a party with an important interest in the decision that is made. For example, if the court is considering a case between the government and a petroleum company, amicus curiae briefs may be submitted by other petroleum companies, state governments, environmental organizations, etc.

Appellate jurisdiction The authority of a court to hear an appeal of a decision from a lower court. Appellate courts do not conduct trials; instead they review the record of the original trial to determine if the law was interpreted and applied correctly. In the federal court system, U.S. Courts of Appeals have appellate jurisdiction. The Supreme Court is the final court of appeal in the federal court system.

Brief A written statement by a party in a court case stating the legal arguments for the decision it is asking the court to make

Civil law Laws governing the relations between private parties where no criminal act is involved. These cases are between two citizens or legal entities and the government is usually not a party in the case.

Concurring opinion A written opinion of one or more justices agreeing with the decision made by the majority, but disagreeing on the legal basis for that decision.

Criminal law Laws making an act (from jaywalking or murder) illegal and punishable by the government. The government charges a person with a crime and is a party in the case.

Dissenting opinion A written opinion of one of more justices disagreeing with the decision of the majority. There may be more than one dissenting opinion in a case.

Judicial activism The doctrine of judicial activism holds that the courts should not be subservient to the other branches of government and should take action when the elected leaders have failed to uphold the Constitution. The Warren Court (1953–1969) is often given as an example of judicial activism. Its decision in *Brown v. Board of Education* is an example of judicial activism in that it overturned precedent and established new national policy while elected officials ignored the problem of racial discrimination.

Judicial restraint The doctrine of judicial restraint holds that judges should not make new national policies through court cases but instead abide by precedent and defer to elected leaders to make national policies.

Judicial review The power of the Supreme Court to declare laws passed by Congress or executive actions of the president unconstitutional. This power is not written into the Constitution but was established by the Supreme Court itself in *Marbury v. Madison* (1803). The Supreme Court functions as the final interpreter of federal law and the Constitution; this allows it to check the power of the president and Congress.

Jurisdiction The authority of a court to hear a case. Federal courts only have jurisdiction in cases involving federal law or the U.S. Constitution.

State laws are interpreted and applied by state courts. If a case only involves state law, the final court of appeal is the state's supreme court. However, federal courts can declare state laws unconstitutional if they violate federal law or the Constitution.

Majority opinion The written opinion in a Supreme Court case signed by a majority of the justices. This becomes the court's decision and serves as a precedent for future cases.

Original jurisdiction The authority of a court to conduct the initial trial of a case. The court with original jurisdiction is called the trial court. It conducts the initial trial, usually with witnesses, lawyers, juries, and a judge. In the federal court system, U.S. District Courts have original jurisdiction.

Plurality opinion In some cases there is no majority opinion (requiring the support of five of the nine justices); the case is decided by the majority of justices who agree on a decision but disagree on the legal basis for that decision. In effect, there are two or more concurring opinions. The concurring opinion with the most signers is the plurality opinion.

Precedent A decision in a previous case that is similar to a case being considered by a court. Courts are generally expected to follow precedents in making their decisions. The Supreme Court can overturn a precedent.

Procedural law Laws governing the legal process itself.

The Supreme Court The final court of appeal in the federal court system. It has appellate jurisdiction, but in some circumstances, such as cases between two state governments, the Court also has original jurisdiction.

U.S. Courts of Appeals The middle layer in the federal court system. U.S. Courts of Appeals have only appellate jurisdiction. They hear cases appealed from U.S. District Courts.

U.S. District Courts The entry level into the federal court system. District courts have original jurisdiction. Cases involving federal law or the Constitution generally begin in U.S. District Courts.

Writ of certiorari If an appellate court decides there are grounds to consider a case, it issues a **writ of certiorari** to the lower court asking it to turn over the records of the case for the appellate court's review.

Writ of habeas corpus Refers to the legal action of challenging one's imprisonment by asking a higher court to review the record of the trial to determine if the law was correctly interpreted and applied. For example, if a person is found guilty on the basis of a state law in a state court, the person can file a writ of habeas corpus, asking a federal court to review the case in light of federal law or the U.S. Constitution.

CIVIL LIBERTIES

Bill of Rights The first ten amendments to the U.S. Constitution, which state rights of the individual and require the government to uphold these rights. In order to get enough support to ratify the Constitution, Federalists agreed that, once the Constitution was ratified, they would work with the Anti-Federalists to add a statement of rights. The process to amend the Constitution to add the Bill of Rights was completed in 1791.

Cruel and unusual punishment The Eighth Amendment prohibits the government's use of "cruel and unusual punishment." However, since what constitutes cruel and unusual punishment is highly subjective, the federal courts have generally allowed Congress and state legislatures to set punishments. Recently, however, the Supreme Court has used the constitutional prohibition of cruel and unusual punishment to overturn state laws applying the death penalty to minors and mentally retarded persons.

Due process clause of the Fourteenth Amendment Requires state governments to follow due process of law in legal proceedings that might deprive a person of his or her life, liberty, or property. This clause has been interpreted by the Supreme Court (*Gitlow v. New York*, 1925) to apply the Bill of Rights to state governments.

Due process of law The concept that government must act in a fair matter in accordance with established laws and procedures. The Fifth Amendment requires due process of law in criminal proceedings and in taking private property for public use (eminent domain).

Eminent domain The power of the government to take private property for public use. The Fifth Amendment requires that this can only be done through due process of law and the Sixth Amendment requires just compensation when the power of eminent domain is used.

Establishment clause The establishment clause of the First Amendment prohibits the establishment of a religion by government and has been interpreted by the Supreme Court as creating a "wall of separation between church and state." In *Engel v. Vitale* (1962) the Supreme Court ruled that the recitation of prayers in public schools was a violation of the establishment clause and therefore unconstitutional. Similarly the Court has banned Bible-reading in public schools and religious displays (such as nativity scenes, but not Christmas trees) in government buildings or parks.

Exclusionary rule The legal principle that evidence obtained illegally cannot be used in a trial.

Free-exercise clause The free-exercise clause of the First Amendment grants people the right to exercise the religion of their choice without government interference. In *Wisconsin v. Yoder* (1972), the Supreme Court ruled that Amish families were exempt from a state law requiring children to attend school until they were sixteen years of age because of long-held religious practices that prioritized work, family, and church over a high school education. However, in other cases, an overriding state interest has been deemed by the Court to be more important than the free exercise of religion. For example, the Supreme Court has ruled that government, with its overriding interest in protecting children, can require medical treatment for children with life-threatening illnesses even when providing such treatment violates the parents' religious beliefs and practices.

Freedom of expression Includes the freedoms of speech, press, and assembly, contained in the First Amendment. Freedom of expression is the most basic right since, without this right, a representative democracy can't function and all other rights are endangered. The Supreme Court has vigorously defended the right to freedom of expression, even when it involves expression of views most people find repugnant.

Miranda rule A rule established in *Miranda v. Arizona* (1966) that criminal suspects must be informed of their rights upon arrest, including their right to an attorney and the right to remain silent.

Prior restraint Government prohibition of freedom of expression before the act takes place. In *The New York Times Company v. United States* (1971), the Court ruled that the government could not stop the *New York Times* from publishing the Pentagon Papers (illegally obtained secret government documents revealing that top officials had deceived the public regarding the Vietnam War). Although the *Times* could be held accountable for violation of a law after publication, the Court ruled that a system of "prior restraint" on the press was dangerously close to government censorship and is unconstitutional.

The rights of the accused The rights of those persons accused of a crime are mainly contained in the Fifth and Sixth Amendments of the Bill of Rights. These rights include the right to an attorney, the right to confront witnesses against you, the right to remain silent, the right to a speedy trial, and the right to trial by an impartial jury.

Right to bear arms The interpretation of the Second Amendment is controversial. Until recently, the Supreme Court had held that, due to the wording of the amendment, the right to bear arms was connected to service in a state militia. In *District of Columbia v. Heller* (2008), however, the Court reversed itself and declared a constitutional right to gun ownership independent of being a member of a state militia.

Right to privacy Although no individual right to privacy is specifically stated in the Bill of Rights, the Supreme Court has determined that the freedoms in the Bill of Rights imply an underlying right to privacy. The right to privacy was established in *Griswold v. Connecticut* (1965), which declared a state law prohibiting the use of birth control devices even by married couples unconstitutional. In *Roe v. Wade* (1973), the Supreme Court determined that the right to privacy is "broad enough to encompass a woman's decision on whether or not to terminate a pregnancy." The Court has also applied the right to privacy to sexual relations between consenting adults; in *Lawrence v. Texas* (2003) it ruled that states could not criminalize consensual sex between adults of the same sex, striking down sodomy laws in the thirteen states that still had them.

Symbolic free speech The Supreme Court has declared that freedom of expression includes symbolic free speech (making a statement with symbols rather than speech). In *Texas v. Johnson* (1989), the Supreme Court ruled that flag burning was a form of symbolic free speech protected by the First Amendment and declared a Texas law banning flag burning to be unconstitutional.

Unreasonable searches and seizures The Fourth Amendment establishes the right of the people "to be secure in their persons, houses, paper, and effects against unreasonable searches and seizures." Search warrants, approved by a judge, may only be issued after police describe what they are looking for and show "probable cause" that it's in the place to be searched. Persons can only be stopped when there is probable cause to believe they have committed a crime.

THE STRUGGLE FOR EQUAL RIGHTS

Affirmative action Refers to policies designed to redress past discrimination and increase the number of minorities in higher education, the labor force, and business by granting preferences to minorities. However, affirmative action was considered "reverse discrimination" by whites who found themselves excluded as a result. In *University of California Regents v. Bakke* (1978), the Supreme Court outlawed racial quotas and in subsequent cases has weakened other affirmative action methods so that racial preferences are now generally regarded as unconstitutional with the exception that race may be used as one of a number of factors in college admissions to insure the diversity that encourages learning.

Civil Rights Act of 1964 A law passed by Congress, under its authority to regulate interstate commerce, that banned segregation in private businesses that provided public accommodations (restaurants, stores, hotels, etc.). The law also banned employment discrimination against African Americans and women.

Civil Rights Movement The struggle, especially during the mid-twentieth century, to achieve equal rights for African Americans.

Disenfranchisement The act of taking away the right to vote.

Emancipation Proclamation (1863) An executive order issued by Lincoln during the Civil War that freed the slaves in certain areas of the South in rebellion against the Union. Most slaves in areas under Union control, however, remained slaves.

Equal protection clause of the Fourteenth Amendment The Fourteenth Amendment, ratified in 1868, required states to treat all citizens equally. However, in practice, African Americans were still treated as second-class citizens. In *Plessy v. Ferguson* (1896), the Supreme Court ruled that segregation of blacks in separate facilities did not violate the equal protection clause as long as the facilities were equal. But in actuality, blacks excluded from whites-only facilities seldom had access to equal facilities. In *Brown v. Board of Education* (1954), the Supreme Court reversed itself and declared that separate facilities were inherently unequal and that public schools must be open to all races.

Fifteenth Amendment (1870) Extended the right to vote to African American males. However, state governments in the South soon passed laws that had the effect of disenfranchising (see above) many African Americans.

Literacy test Many states in the South instituted literacy tests that citizens were required to pass in order to exercise their right to vote. Like the poll tax, literacy tests were used to disenfranchise African Americans. Literacy tests were eliminated by the Voting Rights Act (1965).

Nineteenth Amendment (1920) This amendment granted suffrage to women, ending election laws that restricted voting to males.

Poll tax A tax on voting. This tax was used to disenfranchise African Americans, as well as low-income whites, who could not afford the tax. The poll tax was eliminated by the Twenty-fourth Amendment (1964).

Racial Segregation Separation of races, which can be due to law (**de jure segregation**) or due to tradition or even choice (**de facto segregation**).

Suffrage The right to vote. **Universal suffrage** refers to the situation in which all adults have the right to vote.

Thirteenth Amendment (1865) Ended slavery in the United States.

Voting Rights Act of 1965 A law that outlawed discriminatory voting practices, including literacy tests, that had been used to disenfranchise African Americans in the South. In addition, states with histories of discriminatory practices were to be monitored by the federal government to make sure they didn't continue to use discriminatory voting practices.

Women's suffrage movement The political movement started in the mid-1800s whose goal was to achieve the right to vote for women, which was accomplished in 1920 with the passage of the Nineteenth Amendment.

POLITICAL PARTIES AND ELECTIONS

Blanket primary Primary election in which all parties' candidates are listed on one ballot. Voters may vote for one candidate for each office, crossing party lines if they wish, with the winning candidate in each party becoming the party's candidate in the general election. The blanket primary was declared unconstitutional by the Supreme Court (*California Democratic Party v. Jones*, 2000) on the grounds that it violates the party's right to choose its own candidates.

Closed primary Primary election in which only voters registered as members of a political party may vote.

Electoral college The body that officially selects the president. Each state gets the same number of electors as it has senators and representatives in Congress. Electors are selected by the popular vote for president in each state, with most states using a winner-take-all rule. It takes the votes of a majority of electors to select the president. If no one candidate gets this number (there's a tie or multiple candidates obtained electoral votes denying anyone a majority), the House of

Representatives selects the president from the top three persons in the Electoral College vote. Due largely to the winner-take-all rule, the vote in the Electoral College seldom closely reflects the popular vote for president and occasionally a president is selected that did not obtain the largest popular vote (most recently in 2000).

Electoral realignment A realignment of the groups that form the coalitions supporting each major party. Electoral realignment generally occurs in times of national upheaval, such as the Civil War, which resulted in the Republican Party becoming the majority party, and the Great Depression, which produced FDR's Democratic New Deal Coalition. The passage of the Civil Rights Act of 1964 produced an electoral realignment in the South, which went from solidly Democratic to Republican-leaning.

General election The election in which the winning candidate is chosen for public office. All political parties are on one ballot. General elections for federal offices are held on the Tuesday following the first Monday of November in even-numbered years.

Midterm elections Federal elections held in years when there is no presidential election. These elections happen in the middle of a president's four-year term of office.

Minor (or "third") parties In the American two-party system, minor parties are usually called "third" parties. Third parties seldom mount credible campaigns. Occasionally a third party, usually organized around a single issue or a single popular candidate, gets a significant share of the vote, but rarely do third parties have much influence in U.S. government. At the time of publication, only one of 435 members of the House of Representatives was a member of a third party.

National party convention Political party conventions held every four years for the purpose of choosing the party's candidate for president. The presidential candidate who is selected then chooses the vice presidential candidate.

Nonpartisan blanket primary Similar to the blanket primary, but instead of choosing winning candidates of each party, the nonpartisan blanket primary simply selects two candidates to run in the general election. The two winning candidates may be independents, from different parties, or even from the same political party. The Supreme Court has upheld this type of primary election, which has the effect of eliminating political party control of the candidate selection process, although a party may still endorse candidates if it chooses. This system is currently used in California and Washington State as well as in primary elections for state offices in Louisiana.

Open primary Primary election in which voters may choose which party's election they want to participate in. It is not necessary to be registered as a member of a political party to vote in its primary election.

Party caucuses Party meetings at the local precinct level through which delegates to national party conventions are selected in states that do not have presidential preference primaries.

Political party An organized coalition of interests that works together under a common party label to elect politicians supportive of their interests and views.

Presidential preference primaries Most delegates to national party conventions are selected through presidential preference primary elections. State presidential preference primaries begin in February and go into June of a presidential election year.

Primary election An election in which voters select a political party's candidates for public offices (one candidate is selected to be the party's candidate for each office). The winning candidates from each party's primary election run against each other in the general election. Primary elections are held on dates set by state governments.

Ticket-splitting Voting for a member of one party for one office and a member of another party for another office on the same ballot.

Two-party system A political system dominated by two major political parties competing for power. Since the Civil War, the Democratic and Republican Parties have competed for power in the United States.

INTEREST GROUPS

Grass-roots lobbying Efforts by interest groups to organize their members to contact their representatives in Congress regarding proposed legislation. Grass-roots lobbying is used to help convince members of Congress that the people of their district support the interest group's position and will be watching how their representative votes. If a sufficient number of individuals get involved, grass-roots lobbying can be very effective in helping the interest group influence legislation.

Interest group (also called **pressure groups** or **special interests**) People organized to promote a common political interest. Interest groups can be business groups (U.S. Chamber of Commerce, the Association of Wheat Growers), professional/labor groups (American Medical Association, AFL-CIO), or citizen groups (National Rifle Association, League of Women Voters, Sierra Club).

Iron triangle A network of well-positioned people—representing Congress, federal agencies, and the interest group itself—who work together to promote the policy goals of an interest group. If an interest group can build such a network among the leaders of the congressional committees and the federal agencies that are key to its goals, the interest group can wield considerable power and influence.

Lobbying The efforts made by interest groups to influence public officials. Interest groups can influence public officials by providing information to lawmakers and federal agencies, endorsing candidates and raising campaign funds, and undertaking public relations campaigns to influence public opinion (including advertising on television).

Lobbyist A person employed by an interest group to engage in lobbying. The most effective lobbyists are the ones with the best access to public officials.

Pluralism Term used to describe political systems in which a large number of interest groups compete to form public policies. The **theory of pluralism** holds that society's interests as a whole are served through this process of competition among multiple special interests, since it leads to compromise because no one special interest can gain power over all the others.

Political Action Committee (PAC) A committee formed, usually by an interest group or business corporation, to raise campaign funds and distribute them to selected candidates supportive of the group's positions. Interest groups and businesses are generally prohibited by law from using their own contributions and membership fees for political contributions; they can, however, raise money for politicians through PACs.

Political gridlock Describes the situation when no interest group has the power needed to realize its policy goals, but does have the power to block competing interest groups from achieving their policy goals. Thus gridlock results with nothing getting done, especially in Congress where a supermajority is required to pass laws.

POLITICAL CULTURE AND THE MASS MEDIA

Capitalism (also known as the **free enterprise system**) An ideology based on the belief that government should not become involved in the economy because the good of society is served by allowing businesses to compete with each other as they try to maximize profits.

Ideology A core system of political values and beliefs that influences a person's political positions and opinions. Different ideologies exist within a political culture.

Liberal versus conservative In American politics, someone identifying as a liberal is likely to favor government involvement in the economy and government action to deal with social problems. A conservative is likely to be suspicious of government programs and opposed to the taxation needed to carry them out. Conservatives are less supportive of government involvement in the regulating business and the economy. Applied to social issues, the terms *liberal* and *conservative* take on other meanings. A social conservative supports government action to uphold traditional religious and social practices and beliefs while a social liberal is more likely to be supportive of things like abortion and GLBT rights. Not all liberals are social liberals and not all conservatives are social conservatives.

Libertarianism An ideology based on the belief that individuals and businesses should have as much freedom as possible over their own behavior and that federal government should be cut way back to a much smaller organization that does not get involved in things such as social security or education.

News media All the forms of news communication that reach large segments of the public, including newspapers, magazines, books, television, radio, and the Internet. In a democracy, the mass media perform the functions of informing the public, focusing public attention on an issue or event (thus helping to set the national agenda), uncovering scandal and malfeasance, and providing a vehicle for individuals (including politicians) to express their views and beliefs.

Objective journalism Reporting of the news that is based on facts, presents opposing viewpoints, and does not promote a particular political view or position.

Partisan journalism News reporting or commentary that advocates or supports a particular political party or position.

Political alienation A feeling of powerlessness based on the belief that a person can't make a difference in politics. Both political apathy and political alienation generally lead to noninvolvement in voting and politics.

Political apathy A feeling of not caring about politics and the belief that political involvement isn't important

Political culture The political values and beliefs shared by a people. American political culture is characterized by beliefs—such as majority rule, limited government, individual (natural) rights, and freedom of expression—that are widely shared by people across the political spectrum. A country's political system is based on its political culture.

Political socialization The process through which people acquire their political opinions, beliefs, and values. The most important influences in political socialization are the family, school, peer group, church (or other religious organization), and the mass media.

The press News organizations and the journalists who work for them are collectively referred to as "the press." In the United States, the press consist primarily of privately owned for-profit companies.

Socialism An ideology based on the belief that government should have a strong role in the economy rather than leaving it to privately owned businesses seeking their own profit. Socialists favor government control or ownership of business and industry.

Topic 1: The Constitution and the Basic Principles of American Government

> Before tackling this in-depth review, make sure you've read Big Ideas 2, 3, and 4 and reviewed the key terms relating to the Constitution and the basic principles of American government.

1. What are the classic forms of government?

Aristotle's classification of governments in ancient Greece is still widely used today. Even the actual English-language words come from ancient Greece.

- **Anarchy** is the absence of government.
- **Autocracy** describes a government in which one person holds the power, such as an **absolute monarchy** or **dictatorship**.
- **Oligarchy** refers to a government in which a few people (an elite) control the government.
- **Democracy** is rule by many people; in ancient Athens that was adult males, excluding slaves.

2. What are different types of democratic government?

Direct democracy is government by the people themselves assembled in a meeting passing laws for their community by a majority vote. Direct democracy also applies the **initiative** process in some states (like

California) in which the people can pass laws in a statewide election. In a **representative democracy**, the people don't vote on laws but for representatives who make the laws. A **constitutional democracy** refers to a country governed by a constitution that establishes some type of a representative democracy. A **constitutional monarchy** is similar to a constitutional democracy but there is still a monarch who has little or no power but serves as a symbolic head of state.

3. What are the most important theories of modern democratic government?

Traditional democratic theory holds that "the people" govern through their elected representatives. But most political scientists, who look more at real-world behavior than constitutions, realize that doesn't accurately describe what really happens. **Pluralist theory** holds that the American political process is better described by the competition among numerous special interest groups each seeking their own political goals, resulting in bargaining and compromise to produce public policy. **Elite theory** holds that, in reality, the American political process is dominated by wealthy, well-educated elites who determine public policy. **Bureaucratic theory** holds that the political process is dominated by the vast bureaucracy, which, in promoting its own interests and goals, develops and delivers public policy.

4. How does the Constitution differ from the Articles of Confederation?

The Constitutional Convention was called because there was a broad consensus that a stronger national government was needed. The chart below compares the national governments created under each of these documents.

THE CONSTITUTION AND THE ARTICLES OF CONFEDERATION

The Articles of Confederation	The Constitution
Created a "league of friendship" in which state governments retained sovereignty	Created a system of shared sovereignty between the federal government and state governments
All power vested in the Continental Congress—no branches of government	Three independent branches of government (separation of powers)
National government had no power of taxation; to raise funds, it had to ask the states for contributions.	Congress explicitly given the power to raise and collect taxes
No mechanism for settling disputes between states	The Supreme Court given original jurisdiction to hear disputes between state governments
A unicameral legislature in which each state, regardless of size, had one vote	A bicameral legislature—in one house each state has equal representation (Senate) while in the other representation is apportioned based on population (House of Representatives).
States controlled foreign and interstate commerce and coined their own money.	Federal government granted power to control interstate and foreign commerce and create a national currency
Individual states able to sign treaties with foreign countries and enter in wars	Federal government given control of foreign affairs; state governments prohibited from signing treaties or engaging in war with foreign countries
No process for admitting new states to the union	Created rules for admitting new states to the union
Unanimous consent of states required to amend Articles	Constitution more easily amended although a two-thirds majority of both houses of Congress and approval by three-fourths of states required

5. What are the basic principles contained in the Constitution and Bill of Rights?

Among the principles embodied in the Constitution are the following:

- Limited Government
- Representative Government
- Popular Sovereignty
- Separation of Powers
- Checks and Balances
- Federalism
- Civil Liberties

See also: Big Ideas 1, 2, 3, 4, 5 (pages 5–13)

6. What checks and balances are included in the Constitution?

The chart below summarizes the most important checks that each branch of government has on the other branches.

IMPORTANT CHECKS ON THE POWERS OF OTHER BRANCHES

Congress Checks...	
The Executive Branch	**The Judicial Branch**
Congress can override a veto.	Congress must approve nominations of federal judges when vacancies occur.
The Senate must approve presidential nominees for judges, ambassadors, and key officials of the executive branch.	Congress can initiate Constitutional amendments to overturn Supreme Court decisions.
The Senate must ratify all treaties negotiated by the president by a two-thirds majority.	Congress can rewrite legislation declared unconstitutional by the Supreme Court.
Congress can hold public hearings and investigate actions taken by the executive branch.	Congress decides the size, structure, and jurisdictions of lower federal courts.

Congress can pass a law to overturn an executive order or federal regulation.	Congress can impeach federal judges and remove them from office.
Congress can restrict what the president and the federal bureaucracy can do by refusing to appropriate money for a program, agency, war, etc.	
Congress can impeach the president and remove him from office.	

The President Checks...

The Legislative Branch	The Judicial Branch
The president can veto legislation passed by Congress.	The president nominates federal judges.
The president executes laws passed by Congress, giving him influence over their interpretation and implementation.	The president executes Supreme Court decisions, giving him or her influence over their implementation.
The president can recommend legislation and call a special session of Congress.	The president can pardon individuals convicted of a crime.

The Supreme Court Checks...

The Legislative Branch	The Executive Branch
The Supreme Court can declare a law to be unconstitutional, thereby invalidating the law.	The Supreme Court can declare a federal regulation written by a federal agency to be contrary to either federal law or the U.S. Constitution, thereby invalidating the regulation.
	The Supreme Court can declare an action or executive order of the president to be contrary to either federal law or the U.S. Constitution, thereby invalidating the order.

7. How can the Constitution be amended?

Article V of the Constitution creates a process to amend the Constitution. Congress, by a two-thirds majority in both houses of Congress, can propose amendments to the Constitution. Alternatively, amendments can be proposed by a national constitutional convention if two-thirds of the states pass resolutions calling for such a convention. Any amendment must be approved by three-fourths of the states, either by the state legislature or a state constitutional convention. The president has no role in the process and the people never vote on constitutional amendments.

8. What are the important amendments to the Constitution?

Some amendments are relatively minor; for example, the Twenty-seventh Amendment only concerns when pay raises for members of Congress take effect. Other amendments don't really apply to this century; for example, the Third Amendment prohibits quartering of soldiers in private homes without the owner's consent.

IMPORTANT CONSTITUTIONAL AMENDMENTS

Amendments Stating Individual Rights		
1st	Freedom of expression and freedom of religion	1791
2nd	Right to bear arms	1791
4th	Freedom from unreasonable searches and seizures	1791
5th	Right of the accused: right to remain silent, right to due process of law	1791
6th	Rights of the accused: right to have an attorney, right to a speedy and public trial, right to an impartial jury	1791
8th	Freedom from cruel and unusual punishment	1791
Amendments Extending Rights to Minorities		
13th	Ended slavery	1865
14th	Required states to provide due process of law and equal protection of the law to all their citizens	1868
15th	Prohibited states from denying the right to vote on the grounds of race	1870
19th	Extended the right to vote to women	1920
24th	Eliminated poll tax	1964
26th	Lowered the minimum age for voting to eighteen years	1971
Amendments Changing Governmental Institutions		
17th	Required election of senators by the people rather than state legislatures	1913
22nd	Limited president to two terms in office	1951
25th	Set process for filling the office of vice president if the office is vacant and defined what happens if president is incapacitated and can't perform duties	1967
Amendments Changing Public Policy		
16th	Gave Congress the power to levy taxes based on income	1913
18th	Prohibited production and sale of alcoholic beverages	1919
21st	Repealed the Eighteenth Amendment	1933

Landmark Supreme Court Decisions

Marbury v. Madison (1803) The Supreme Court's decision in this case established the principle of **judicial review**—the Court's power to declare laws passed by Congress unconstitutional. This power is not written into the Constitution but was established by the precedent of this case. In *Marbury v. Madison*, which actually concerned only a minor procedural manner of commissioning a justice of the peace, the Supreme Court stated that it is the final interpreter of the law and the Constitution. The principle of judicial review applies, not just to laws passed by Congress, but also laws passed by state legislatures and actions of the federal and state executive branches.

McCulloch v. Maryland (1819) This decision is really two landmark cases in one. It established the supremacy of the federal government over state governments and it established a broad interpretation of the "necessary and proper" clause (Article I, Section 8). This case arose from the refusal of an official of the Baltimore branch of the Bank of the United States (established by the federal government) to pay a tax levied by Maryland on activities of the bank. First, the Court ruled that the establishment of the Bank of the United States was constitutional—even though the establishment of a national bank was not among the powers expressly granted Congress—due to the "necessary and proper" clause, which states that Congress has the power "to make all Laws which shall be necessary and proper for carrying into execution" the powers expressly granted to Congress. Then, the Court held that Maryland could not impose a tax on the bank because state governments cannot "retard, impede, burden, or in any manner control the operation of the constitutional laws enacted by Congress" due to Article VI, which states that federal law is to be supreme over state law.

Topic 1 Review

1. In *Marbury v. Madison,* the Supreme Court

  A. reaffirmed the principle of judicial review stated in the Constitution

  B. reestablished the supremacy of the federal government over state governments

  C. established the precedent that the Supreme Court could declare bills passed by Congress unconstitutional before the president signs them making them law

  D. established the precedent that the Supreme Court can void laws it determines are unconstitutional

  E. established that the federal government had "implied powers"

2. Congress can check the power of the president by all of the following means EXCEPT

  A. overriding a veto

  B. rejecting a nominee for federal judge

  C. nominating a Supreme Court Justice the president does not approve

  D. rejecting a treaty

  E. appropriating money for a weapons system the president does not support

3. The idea that the government should consist of independent branches is known as

  A. checks and balances

  B. separation of powers

  C. federalism

  D. popular sovereignty

  E. representative government

4. Constitutionalism is the principle that asserts that

  A. government is divided into three branches, each performing its own function

  B. a system of checks and balances should protect the people from the abuse of power

  C. government should be based on a written constitution approved by the people

  D. the federal government's power is supreme over state governments

  E. the power of government is limited to the powers it has been given

Topic 2: Federalism

Before tackling this in-depth review, make sure you've read
Big Idea 1 and reviewed the key terms relating to federalism.

1. How is power divided between state and federal governments?

For most of U.S. history, there was thought to be a fairly clear division of powers between federal and state governments.

- **Federal powers** These powers include the powers specifically expressed in Article I, Section 8, of the Constitution, including providing for the common defense, regulating interstate and foreign commerce, coining money, collecting taxes, etc. These are called **the expressed, enumerated,** or **delegated powers.** In addition, federal government has **implied powers**—the power to make "necessary and proper" laws for carrying out the expressed powers, a provision that has been broadly interpreted by the Supreme Court.

- **State powers** State powers are called **reserved powers**. These are powers reserved for state governments under the Tenth Amendment, which states that "Powers not delegated to the United States by the Constitution...are reserved to the States." Traditionally these have included the power to regulate intrastate commerce (commerce within a state), establish local governments, administer elections, establish public school systems, regulate corporations, and make traffic laws. Today, although state governments still play the predominant administrative role in these areas, the federal government, primarily through the requirements accompanying federal grants, also has a strong influence and can often set and enforce national policies.

- **Concurrent powers** Powers that both the federal government and state governments have. These include the power to levy taxes, borrow money, establish court systems, charter banks, investigate crimes, etc.

- **Prohibited powers** Powers prohibited to state or federal governments by the Constitution. For example, state governments cannot coin money, sign treaties with foreign governments, tax imports (tariffs), or interfere with the enforcement of contracts. Neither state nor federal governments can grant titles of nobility, pass ex post facto laws (laws making an act a crime even though it wasn't a crime at the time it was committed), or tax exports.

2. What happens when state governments and the federal government collide?

When people don't like the policies of the national government, they often take up the cause of states' rights, holding that the national government is usurping the powers of the states. Usually disputes about the proper division of power between state and federal governments are settled in the courts. However, a few times in U.S. history, the struggle between advocates of states' rights and those who support the federal government has exploded.

Nullification (1832) The doctrine of nullification (most forcibly espoused by John C. Calhoun of South Carolina) held that, since it was the states who came together to form the United States, the United States was a "government of states" in which each state was still sovereign within its own territory. In 1832, South Carolina, using the doctrine of nullification, passed a law declaring a tariff law passed by federal government "null and void" within the state. President Andrew

Jackson called South Carolina's position "incompatible with the existence of the Union" and threatened to send federal troops to South Carolina, a threat Congress backed up with an authorization for the use of military force against the state. The state government backed down, but only after Congress amended the tariff law to soften its impact on the South.

Secession (1861) The doctrine of secession held that, since the states had voluntarily joined the United States, they could voluntarily leave it as well. After the election of Abraham Lincoln in 1860, eleven southern state governments declared they were seceding from the United States. This led to the Civil War, which, of course, the secessionist states lost. The northern states supported the **doctrine of an indestructible union,** which held that the states had formed a union that was greater than the sum of the parts and that this union, as Abraham Lincoln said, could not be "torn asunder."

States' rights (1957) The doctrine of states' rights was used by several southern governors who refused to obey court orders requiring the racial integration of public schools following *Brown v. Board of Education* (1954). They held that operating school systems was a power reserved for the states in which the federal government had no power to intervene. In 1957 nine African Americans attempted to enroll in all-white Central High School in Little Rock, Arkansas. The Arkansas governor deployed the Arkansas National Guard to block the students' entry. President Eisenhower federalized the Arkansas National Guard, putting it under his control (a power derived from Article II of the Constitution), and sent federal troops (the 101st Airborne Division of the U.S. Army) to protect the nine students and permit them to enter the school. The state government of Arkansas was forced to back down.

3. How does the Constitution regulate relations between states?

"Full faith and credit" clause (Article IV) The Constitution requires that states recognize the "Acts, Records, and judicial Proceedings of every other state." For example, if two people marry in one state, they are considered married even if they cross into another state. In reality, problems result when the act of one state is not legal in another state. Thus, interracial marriages were not recognized by many southern states until the Supreme Court's ruling in *Loving v. Virginia*, and the Court has not ruled on whether this clause requires all states to recognize same-sex marriages legally performed in the states that allow them.

"**Privileges and immunities" clause** (Article IV) States are prohibited from discriminating against citizens of other states. For example, a U.S. citizen may own property in any state, travel freely in any state, work in another state (if licensing requirements are met), etc. The Supreme Court, however, has ruled that certain out-of-state fees such as out-of-state tuition and a higher fee for hunting licenses for out-of-state residents are legal.

4. What are the leading theories of federalism today?

Dual federalism, the traditional way of looking at federalism, is largely outmoded and the theories of **fiscal federalism** and **cooperative federalism** are the most common theories used to describe the operation of federalism today. All three of these are defined and explained in the Key Terms and also discussed under Big Idea 1 (federalism) on page 5.

5. What types of grants does the federal government give state and local governments?

Federal grants to state and local governments have grown considerably and now constitute an important part of state government revenues. Federal grants to state and local governments are one way the federal government makes and enforces national policies.

- **Grants-in-aid** are federal cash payments to state and local governments for projects that they carry out and programs that they administer.

- **Categorical grants** are federal grants to state or local governments that fund a specific project or program. They usually come with many requirements attached. Categorical grants may be in the form of a **project**

grant, which is awarded on the basis of a competitive application. State or local governments must apply for funding and often matching funds from the state or local government are required. **Formula grants**, on the other hand, do not require grant applications; they are awarded on the basis of a legal formula set by Congress. Medicaid is an example of a formula grant. Most federal grants to state and local governments are categorical grants and most of these are project grants.

- **Block grants** are federal grants to state and local governments that can be used for programs in a broad policy area such as education or law enforcement, rather than for a specific project. They give state and local governments more freedom to decide how federal funds are spent. No grant application is needed; instead, block grants are awarded to states on the basis of a formula set by Congress.

6. How do federal grants influence national policy?

Federal grants to state and local governments usually come with many requirements attached. For example, the federal government required state governments to raise the legal drinking age to twenty-one (in some states it was only eighteen) in order for the state to continue receiving federal highway grants. In theory, a state has the freedom to refuse federal funding and leave the legal drinking age at eighteen. But in reality, refusing significant federal highway funding is not in any state's interest and all states quickly complied with the policy and set the drinking age at twenty-one. Setting the legal drinking age is a matter traditionally left to state governments; however, through the use of federal grants to state governments, the federal government was able to set and enforce a national policy on this issue.

Landmark Supreme Court Decisions

McCulloch v. Maryland (1819) This is the most important Supreme Court decision regarding the relationship between federal and state governments. Be sure to review the description of this case provided at the end of Topic I on page 92.

Gibbons v. Ogden (1824) In this decision, the Supreme Court held that a New York law granting a monopoly to a New York company on ferry service between New York and New Jersey was unconstitutional. The Court held that the law interfered with the federal government's power to control interstate commerce. The power to control interstate commerce, the Court ruled, was exclusively a federal power and state governments could not get involved in regulating or restricting interstate commerce.

Dartmouth College v. Woodward (1819) This decision of the Supreme Court held that the state government of New Hampshire could not unilaterally change Dartmouth College's charter to make the college a public college rather than a private one. The Court based its decision on Article I, Section 9, which prohibits states from passing a law "impairing the Obligation of Contracts." The college's charter was a contract and changing it without Dartmouth's consent was a power prohibited state governments by the Constitution.

Coyle v. Smith (1911) The Supreme Court upheld the right of the state of Oklahoma to change the location of its state capital, declaring a provision in the federal law admitting Oklahoma as a state to be unconstitutional. Federal law has supremacy over state law (Article VI) but, according to the Court, determining the location of the state capital is clearly not a power of the federal government, but a power reserved for the states.

Hicklin v. Orbeck (1978) The Supreme Court's decision used the "privileges and immunities" clause of Article IV to declare unconstitutional an Alaska law requiring oil and gas companies doing business within the state to give preference to local residents in hiring employees. The court determined this law discriminated against citizens of other states and was therefore unconstitutional.

Topic 2 Review

1. The idea that federal and state governments each have their own policy areas that they control is called

   A. fiscal federalism
   B. dual federalism
   C. cooperative federalism
   D. reserved powers
   E. delegated powers

2. The power to levy taxes is

   A. a concurrent power
   B. an implied power
   C. a reserved power
   D. fiscal federalism
   E. monetary policy

3. Which of the following was NOT an outcome of the Supreme Court's *McCulloch v. Maryland* (1819) decision?

   A. the establishment of the precedent of judicial review
   B. the establishment of the supremacy of the federal government over state governments
   C. the declaration that state governments could not tax or interfere with federal programs
   D. the affirmation that the federal government has implied powers not specifically stated in the Constitution
   E. the declaration that Congress had the power to establish a national bank

4. Devolution is the idea that

    A. the Constitution should be amended to give the states more power

    B. Congress should be prohibited from passing laws that create unfunded mandates for state governments

    C. state governments should not be required to follow federal regulations

    D. the federal government should become more involved in policy areas such as education that have been traditionally controlled by state governments

    E. the federal government should give more power to state governments in administering federal programs

Topic 3: Congress:
The Legislative Branch

Before tackling this in-depth review, make sure you've read Big Ideas 2, 3, and 9 and reviewed the key terms relating to Congress and the legislative branch.

1. What roles do members of Congress (senators and representatives) play?

There are four important roles that define the job of senators and representatives:

1. **Legislative role** The members of Congress perform the legislative function of passing the laws that govern the United States.
2. **Role of representation** Members of Congress also perform the function of representing their constituents in the national government, which requires expressing their views and looking after their interests, including getting federal money for funds for projects in their districts. It's important to understand that this role of representing constituents may clash with the legislative role of a member of Congress. This happens when the opinions or interests of the constituency conflict with what the senator or representative believes to be in the interest of the nation as a whole. In making laws, should the senator or representative represent his/her constituency or do what he/she believes best for the country as a whole?

3. **Role of providing constituent services** (also known as constituent casework) Senators and representatives devote most of the time of their office staff to helping individual constituents with problems they are having relating to federal government agencies. By providing good constituent services, members of Congress improve their reelection prospects by gaining the gratitude of the constituents who've been helped.

4. **Oversight role** Congress, in addition to passing laws, also performs an oversight function. It oversees the executive branch and investigates situations in which federal officials or agencies may be involved in misconduct or improper behavior. Usually this is done by holding congressional hearings that expose the misconduct to the public.

2. What does the Constitution say about how Congress operates?

Most of the Constitution deals with Congress (Article I). It describes the division of Congress into two houses, how members of Congress are selected, what powers it has, and what powers it does not have. However, the Constitution does not describe the legislative process. Instead, it stipulates that each house of Congress make its own rules regarding how the legislative process will operate. Only one constitutional amendment directly relates to Congress. The **Seventeenth Amendment** (1913) changes the way senators are chosen; now they are elected by the people of the state rather than the state legislature.

3. Who leads Congress?

The leadership of both houses of Congress is fragmented; in other words, no one leader, with the possible exception of the Speaker of the House, has much power. Power is divided among the chairs of standing committees (of which there are thirty-seven), each with considerable power in the area of the committee's jurisdiction. No person, not even the Speaker of the House—whose power doesn't extend to the Senate—can speak for Congress as a whole. In fact, one reason the power of Congress has declined relative to the president's power, is Congress's lack of quick, decisive, and effective leadership. Congress is led by a large group of people who seldom agree among themselves on any issue.

Following are the most important figures in Congress:

- **Speaker of the House** The Speaker of the House is the presiding officer of the House of Representatives and the party leader of the majority party in the House. The Speaker is selected by the majority party caucus, which then votes as a block to get the person elected by the entire House of Representatives. The Speaker of the House is the most powerful member of the House.

- **Majority Leader** In the Senate, the leader of the majority party is the most powerful senator. In the House, the person elected to this position is actually second in command after the Speaker of the House, who functions as the leader of the majority party. Majority leaders are elected by members of the majority party in their party caucus.

- **Minority Leader** In both the Senate and House, the minority leader is the leader of minority party and is elected by the members of the minority party.

- **President of the Senate** The vice president of the United States has only one constitutional function—other than taking over if the president dies—which is to serve as president of the Senate. However, due to the rules of the Senate, this position has very little power except to break tie votes in the Senate. Thus, the vice president is generally present in the Senate only when there is the possibility of an important vote on legislation ending in a tie.

4. What types of committees are there in Congress?

Both the Senate and the House operate using a similar committee system. The various types of committees are listed below.

- **Standing Committee** A permanent committee that continues from one session of Congress to the next. New members of Congress are assigned to standing committees to fill vacancies left by members of Congress who retired or lost elections. The Senate has seventeen standing committees and the House has twenty. These committees conduct most of the work of Congress, and each committee dominates the legislative process in the area in which it has jurisdiction.

- **Subcommittee** Standing committees are subdivided into subcommittees, each with jurisdiction over a different part of the committee's broad jurisdiction.

- **Conference Committee** A committee composed of members of the House and Senate to reconcile similar bills passed by the Senate and House. When both houses have passed similar bills, a conference committee negotiates a compromise bill that both houses must then approve in order for it to be sent to the president for his signature or veto.

- **Joint Committee** A committee that contains both members of the Senate and members of the House.

- **Select Committee** A temporary committee, as opposed to a standing committee.

5. What are the most powerful committees of Congress?

Each standing committee of Congress has considerable power over legislation in its area of jurisdiction. Among the most powerful standing committees are the following:

- **Rules Committee** The committee of the House of Representatives that decides whether a bill will be considered by the full House and then sets the rules for floor debate, including the time limitations and the number of amendments that can be offered.

- **Ways and Means Committee** The committee of the House of Representatives that considers taxation bills. Taxation bills must begin in the House and cannot be considered by the Senate until they have passed the House. Thus, this committee has a powerful influence on all matters relating to taxation.

- **Appropriations Committees** Both the House and Senate have an Appropriations Committee, whose job is to determine funding for the agencies and programs of the federal government. They have enormous influence over all programs of the federal government and are among the most powerful committees of Congress.

6. How does a bill become a law?

The rules of the Senate and House are complex, and sometimes the legislative process can have unpredictable twists and turns. Below is a summary of the usual process by which a new law is created.

HOW A BILL BECOMES LAW

Step 1	Any member of Congress can introduce a bill. Bills involving taxation, however, can only be introduced by representatives.
Committee Action	
Step 2	The bill is referred to the standing committee with jurisdiction over the subject matter of the bill and then the bill is usually referred to the appropriate subcommittee of the committee. The subcommittee can ignore the bill, thereby killing it; more than 90 percent of bills die at this step of the process.
Step 3	However, if there is sufficient support for the bill, hearings are held in which supporters and opponents of the bill make their case. Experts are asked to testify as well.
Step 4	If there is still sufficient support for the bill, the subcommittee amends the bill as it sees fit and, by majority vote, reports it to the full committee for its consideration.
Step 5	The full committee can ignore the bill, thereby killing it, or decide to consider it. If there is sufficient support, the full committee takes up the bill and usually amends it further. If a majority of the committee supports the bill, the committee reports the bill to the full House or Senate.

Floor Action	
Step 6	The full House or Senate can ignore the bill (if party leaders are opposed or if there is insufficient support), thereby killing the bill. Or party leaders can decide to put it on the calendar for floor debate. In the House, the Rules Committee puts the bill on the calendar and sets the rules for floor debate.
Step 7	The full House or Senate debates the bill and can amend the bill by majority vote.
Step 8	A vote is taken to end debate (cloture) and vote on the bill. In the House cloture is by majority vote but in the Senate sixty senators must support cloture, allowing a filibuster in which a minority can sometimes block passage of a bill supported by the majority by continuing debate indefinitely. If there is not sufficient support to pass a cloture resolution, the bill dies.
Step 9	If the cloture vote passes, a vote is taken on the bill. If a majority oppose the bill, it dies.
Committee and Floor Action in the Other House of Congress	
Step 10	If the bill passes one house of Congress, it goes to the other house, where the same process (steps 2–9) is repeated. At any of these steps, the bill can be killed.
Step 11	If the bill makes it through the other house of Congress and is passed, it usually emerges with at least some provisions that are different from the version that passed the original house. If the bills passed by each house are different, the bill goes to a conference committee.
Conference Committee Action	
Step 12	A conference committee of senators and representatives is appointed to reconcile the different versions of the bill and produce a version both the Senate and House can support.
Floor Action	
Step 13	To move ahead, the exact same bill must be approved by both houses of Congress. If both the House and Senate pass the same version of the bill it goes to the president for his signature.

Presidential Action	
Step 14	The president can sign the bill making it a law, veto the bill, or neither sign nor veto. **If he signs, the bill becomes a law.** If he neither signs nor vetoes the bill, it becomes law ten days later if Congress is still in session. If, however, Congress is not still in session, the bill dies. This is called a pocket veto.
Congressional Action	
Step 15	If the president vetoes the bill, it goes back to Congress, which can override his veto by a two-thirds majority in both houses of Congress. **If Congress overrides his veto, the bill becomes law.**
Step 16	If Congress does not have the votes to override the veto, the bill may die. However, Congress sometimes amends the bill to meet presidential objections and passes it again in its amended form. If an amended bill passes both houses of Congress by majority vote, it goes to the president again for his signature or veto (see step 14).

7. Why is it so difficult for Congress to pass legislation?

There are so many different steps at which proposed legislation can be blocked; if a bill is to keep moving forward, majority support is needed, not just in both houses of Congress but also in a number of committees and subcommittees. Then, because sixty senators are needed for cloture, a minority of forty-one senators can kill a bill through a filibuster. As a result of increasing use of the filibuster, more than a simple majority, often called a "supermajority," is now frequently needed to pass new legislation.

This has often led to **legislative gridlock** in which no party or group—not even a majority party or group—has enough support to pass the legislation it promised. As a result, some have complained that Congress doesn't get much done. In fact, this was the intention of the delegates to the Constitutional Convention (and early senators and representatives who made the rules of the House and Senate that are mostly still in effect today), who distrusted government's power and wanted to make sure the government didn't become tyrannical.

8. What are the biggest influences on Congress?

1. **Interest groups** Interest groups provide information and work closely with senators and representatives that agree with their positions. They endorse members of Congress and urge their members to vote for the candidates they support. However, the real power of interest groups comes from their ability to raise campaign funds; candidates rely on interest groups for much of the money they need to run for election.

2. **Public opinion** Senators and representatives monitor public opinion in their states/districts. They try to stay more or less in step with the view of their constituents, especially on issues that really matter to their states/districts.

3. **Political parties** Not long ago, it used to be that once elected, his/her political party had little influence over how a senator or representative voted. Today, congressional votes increasingly adhere to party lines and senators and representatives can feel enormous pressure from their party's congressional leaders—and the president—to vote with their party.

9. Why is there so little turnover in the members of Congress?

Senators and representatives often get reelected for multiple terms, making a career of being a member of Congress. In fact, in any given federal election 95 percent of representatives and 85 percent of senators are reelected on the average. Incumbents have a big advantage because they generally have greater name recognition, more campaign experience, and better access to media coverage that their challengers usually have. Incumbents also have a clear fundraising advantage, especially with the interest groups whose positions they've supported in Congress. Finally, congressional districts are often drawn in a way that makes them safe for one party or the other. All this means that once you're in Congress, it's hard to get you out.

10. What are the main differences between the House and the Senate?

The table below summarizes the chief differences between the House and Senate. There are also many similarities. Both houses operate under a similar committee system in which leadership is fragmented and committee chairs hold great power. In addition, both houses use a similar process to create new legislation.

THE HOUSE OF REPRESENTATIVES AND THE SENATE

	House of Representatives	Senate
Number of members	435 members	100 members
Term of office	Two years	Six years
Representation of states	Representatives are apportioned to states on the basis of population.	There are two senators from each state regardless of population.
Cloture	Cloture is by majority vote; no filibuster is possible.	Cloture requires sixty senators, making it possible for a minority to block a bill supported by a majority through a filibuster.
Approval of president's nominees for federal office	The House plays no role in approval of presidential appointments.	The Senate must approve president's nominations for federal judges, ambassadors, and key officials of the executive branch.
Approval of treaties	The House plays no role in approval of treaties.	The Senate must approve treaties by two-thirds majority for them to be ratified.

	House of Representatives	Senate
Impeachment	The House has the power to initiate impeachment proceedings and, by majority vote, bring charges against a federal official (including the president and Supreme Court justices).	The Senate tries all impeachments; conviction and removal from office requires a vote by a two-thirds majority.
Presiding officer	Speaker of the House	Vice President of the United States
Electorate	Members are elected by voters in single-member congressional districts.	Members are elected by voters in statewide elections.

Landmark Supreme Court Decisions

***Baker v. Carr* (1962)** The Supreme Court in *Baker v. Carr* required congressional districts within a state to be substantially equal in population ("one man, one vote rule") and that they be redrawn every ten years based on each new federal census. The case was brought by Charles Baker against the State of Tennessee, which had not redistricted since 1901. As a result, the congressional district that included Memphis (where Baker lived) had ten times as many people as the largely rural congressional district in Tennessee with the fewest people. Baker claimed this violated his right to the equal protection of the law guaranteed all citizens in the Fourteenth Amendment. The Court agreed with Baker. In this decision, the Supreme Court reversed an earlier decision that held that redistricting was a legislative matter into which federal courts could not intervene.

***U.S. Term Limits, Inc. v. Thornton* (1995)** In this decision, the Supreme Court unanimously held that according to Article I of the Constitution, the stated restrictions on who can be elected to the Senate and the House were to be the only restrictions; thus, only a constitutional amendment could add more restrictions or qualifications. This ruling invalidated the state laws or state constitutions in twenty-three states that had tried to impose term limits on members of Congress. Ray Thornton, who had already served three terms in the House of Representatives, was blocked from running for reelection by an amendment to the Arkansas Constitution that limited representatives to three terms. U.S. Term Limits, Inc. was an advocacy group that supported the adoption of term limits for members of Congress.

Immigration and Naturalization Service v. Chadha (1983) Until this decision, Congress often wrote into legislation language that gave it power to veto, by passing a congressional resolution, the federal regulations to carry out the law written by the executive branch. The Supreme Court held that such vetoing of a federal regulation was a legislative action equivalent to passing a law, and that under Article II of the Constitution, passing a law requires the signature of the president (or overriding of his veto by Congress). Thus, Congress—acting alone—could not veto or block a federal regulation written by the executive branch to enforce a law; it can only do this by passing new legislation that becomes law when either the president signs it or Congress overrides his veto.

Topic 3 Review

1. Congress performs all the following functions EXCEPT

    A.   passing laws

    B.   constituent casework

    C.   investigating cases of the misuse of power in the executive branch

    D.   deciding how federal funds will be spent

    E.   settling disputes between states

2. Until the Seventeenth Amendment (1913) was ratified, Senators were chosen

    A. by a vote of adult males who held property only

    B. by a vote of adult males only

    C. by state legislatures

    D. by various methods--each state determined how its Senators would be chosen

    E. by the Senate, which selected replacements for retiring Senators

3. Which of the following statements correctly describes redistricting?

    A. Redistricting must be completed before reapportionment can take place.

    B. State governments are responsible for redistricting after seats in the House of Representatives are reapportioned following a national census.

    C. The Supreme Court is responsible for redistricting based on data provided by the census bureau.

    D. Redistricting is carried out by Congress every ten years based on a new national census.

    E. Redistricting can be a determining factor in which party controls both the Senate and House of Representatives.

4. Which of the following does NOT describe Congress?

    A. Congress is bicameral.

    B. Congress is generally slow to act.

    C. A minority in Congress can often block legislation the majority supports.

    D. Congressmen usually represent the broad national interest rather than the narrower interest of their districts/states.

    E. Congress often engages in pork-barrel spending.

Topic 4: The President and the Executive Branch

> Before tackling this in-depth review, make sure you've read Big Ideas 3, 10, 11, 12, and 16 and reviewed the key terms relating to the president and the executive branch.

1. What roles does the president play and how have these roles evolved?

The role of the president has gradually evolved to take on more prominence and power than the writers of the Constitution originally intended. Partly this is due to default; Congress with its fragmented leadership structure cannot act quickly and decisively, leaving only the president with the ability to effectively respond to a crisis. The evolution of presidential power is also the result of the fact that the president is the only federal official chosen by all the people (rather than just those of a single state or congressional district, as members of Congress are). Thus, only the president can speak for the people and claim a mandate to govern. But it wasn't until the twentieth century and the assumption of the presidency by Theodore Roosevelt that the idea of the modern presidency began to emerge. Roosevelt favored an activist presidency in which the president could do whatever he considered necessary to promote the interest of the people as long as he didn't violate federal law or the Constitution. Today, contrary to the intentions of the writers of the Constitution, the president plays the role of national leader in the American political system.

EVOLUTION OF THE ROLE OF THE PRESIDENT

Role	Constitutional Basis	The Modern Presidency
Commander in chief of armed forces	The Constitution names the president commander in chief but gives the power to declare war to Congress. Originally it was envisioned that Congress would decide when the United States goes to war and the president's job would be to carry out the war the Congress declared.	Now the president not only conducts the war, but usually decides when to wage war. Presidents have committed troops to military action abroad more than two hundred times without a declaration of war by Congress.
Chief executive of the U.S. government	The Constitution vests executive power in the president and gives him the power to select key governmental officials subject to Senate approval. Originally it was envisioned that Congress would set national policies and the president would carry them out.	Modern presidents actively use their powers to define national policy, rather than simply serving as an administrator of policies determined by Congress. Presidents hire and fire key officials, issue executive orders, and decide how to interpret and enforce the laws passed by Congress.

Chief diplomat	The Constitution gives the president power to negotiate treaties and nominate ambassadors, giving him the chief tools for carrying out foreign policy. However, the writers of the Constitution believed Congress would determine foreign policy, which the president would simply carry out. Congress must approve the president's nominees for ambassadorships and ratify treaties the president has negotiated by a two-thirds majority.	Today, there is little disagreement that the president, not Congress, is the leader in determining foreign policy. He decides the foreign policy goals of the United States and how to achieve them. The State Department, the Department of Defense, and the CIA are the chief foreign policy vehicles the president has at his disposal. He personally meets foreign leaders and speaks for the United States in the global arena.
Legislator	The writers of the Constitution gave legislative power to Congress and only gave the president a check on this power—the veto. The Constitution also says the president may propose legislation, but he cannot introduce a bill in Congress.	Most presidents since Franklin D. Roosevelt have taken the lead in determining the legislative agenda. Presidents now have a great deal of influence over legislation. This power comes not just from their ability to propose legislation they like and veto legislation they don't like, but also from their modern roles as leader of their political party and an assertive national leader.

2. What other provisions does the Constitution contain regarding the president?

Article II, which defines the presidency and the executive branch, is only about a third the length of Article I, which sets up Congress. Article II includes the following stipulations:

- The president must be at least thirty-five years old, a natural-born citizen of the United States, and a resident of the United States for the fourteen years prior to the election.

- The president is elected by special electors, commonly called the Electoral College, chosen by the winner of the popular vote for president in each state (see Big Idea 16, "Electoral College and the Selection of the President," on page 28).
- The president is chosen for a four-year term of office. The Twenty-second Amendment (1951) limits the president to two terms in office.

3. What other sources of power can the president utilize to lead the nation?

The modern presidency is based on the concept of the president as an activist trying to accomplish his own policy goals, rather than merely carrying out the policies set by Congress. The Constitution gives the president only limited power; his position as leader of the nation is based on powers beyond those specified in the Constitution. Among those factors that have contributed to the president's performing the role of national leader are:

- **National election** The president is the only nationally elected leader, unlike members of Congress, who represent a small minority of the American people. The president also has more freedom than Congress to act quickly and decisively during a crisis.
- **The president as leader of his political party** As the leader of the political party, he can set the party's general priorities and goals and expect that most party members in Congress will follow his lead on most issues.
- **The "bully pulpit"** The president is able to command the attention of the media and the public to promote his vision for the country, his proposed legislation, and even his spin on the opposition party. This ability to get attention is sometimes called the "bully pulpit."
- **Public expectations** The public expects the president to be strong and act decisively when confronted with a crisis or a problem. The widespread "myth of presidential government" (the idea that the president is responsible for all the actions of government) encourages

the president to take strong action, since he can expect to be held accountable for how the nation and its economy are doing.

4. How do the president and Congress interact?

Although the president gets most of the attention, Congress has most of the legislative power. If a president is to get what he wants from Congress, he must be careful to understand and respect the needs of individual members of Congress, including their needs to obtain federal funding for local projects, to demonstrate their importance to constituents, and to assert their independence. If both houses of Congress are controlled by the president's political party, Congress and the president may cooperate to pass new legislation. Vetoes can be expected to be rare in this situation. However, Congress and the president often collide, especially when the president's party does not control both houses of Congress. The ultimate collision between Congress and the president is **impeachment**. A president can be impeached (charged with "high crimes and misdemeanors") by a majority vote in the House of Representatives. This is most likely to happen in a highly polarized political environment as occurred in 1868 with the impeachment of Andrew Johnson and in 1998 with the impeachment of Bill Clinton. To be removed from office, a two-thirds majority of the Senate must find the president guilty. The Senate failed by one vote to remove Andrew Johnson from office and fell seventeen votes short of removing Clinton.

5. What key factors determine how much power a president has?

- **The state of the nation** Much depends on the situation the president inherits or falls into during his term. For example, in his first few months in office Franklin D. Roosevelt accomplished sweeping changes in domestic policy because the nation, deep in the depression, was supportive of dramatic change. When conditions are favorable, the president has great power to bring about change. However, most of the time, circumstances limit the president's power to bring about major changes.

- **The phase of the president's term** The amount of power and influence a president can be expected to exert depends, in part, on the phase of his presidency. During the **honeymoon period**—the first several months of a new president's term in which most problems can be blamed on the previous administration and the new president gets little criticism in the media—the president may be able to successfully make far-reaching changes both by executive order and by pushing legislation through Congress. On the other hand, during the **lame-duck period**— the last year or more of the president's final term in which the president's power is waning since everyone knows he won't be around much longer—few, if any, new presidential policy initiatives can gain traction.

- **Relations with Congress** The amount of power the president can wield depends also on his relations with Congress. For example, Franklin D. Roosevelt was able to dramatically alter domestic policy because his party controlled Congress. If Congress is controlled by the opposition party, the power of the president is reduced and he must settle for much less than he may wish.

- **Public support** Key to the president's ability to wield power and influence is his public support as measured by opinion polls. When the president's public support is high, senators and representatives want to be perceived as supportive of the president; however, when it is low senators and representatives are apt to try to distance themselves from his programs and proposals.

6. How is the federal bureaucracy structured?

Most of the federal bureaucracy falls into fifteen huge departments, each of which consists of many federal agencies and thousands of employees. Each department is headed by a secretary who is a member of the president's cabinet. The secretary is chosen by the president (with Senate approval) and reports to the president.

THE DEPARTMENTS OF THE FEDERAL GOVERNMENT

Executive Department	Department Head	Functions
State	Secretary of State	Runs U.S. embassies, communicates with foreign governments, represents the United States in international organizations, negotiates treaties
Treasury	Secretary of the Treasury	Collect taxes, prints money, manages the national debt
Defense	Secretary of Defense	Runs the army, navy, and air force, operates military bases, procures weapons systems
Interior	Secretary of the Interior	Manages government-owned lands, operates the national parks, manages Native American affairs
Justice	Attorney General	Runs FBI and federal law enforcement agencies, operates federal prisons, represents the U.S. government in court
Agriculture	Secretary of Agriculture	Administers programs for farmers, insures food safety, administers national forests, provides emergency food programs
Commerce	Secretary of Commerce	Conducts census, encourages economic development in the United States, promotes international trade, issues patents
Labor	Secretary of Labor	Enforces labor laws, provides for job training programs, monitors pension plans
Health and Human Services	Secretary of Health and Human Services	Administers welfare programs, conducts medical research, administers Medicare and Medicaid, monitors food and drug safety, controls epidemics

Executive Department	Department Head	Functions
Housing and Urban Development	Secretary of Housing and Urban Development	Administers mortgage assistance programs, manages housing programs for low-income families
Transportation	Secretary of Transportation	Administers programs for highway and mass transit construction, controls air traffic, runs waterways, promotes transportation safety
Energy	Secretary of Energy	Monitors nuclear power facilities, promotes energy conservation, promotes development of new energy technology
Education	Secretary of Education	Administers federal education programs and grants
Veterans Affairs	Secretary of Veterans Affairs	Manages hospitals and benefit programs for veterans
Homeland Security	Secretary of Homeland Security	Operates Coast Guard, patrols borders, provides disaster relief, controls immigration and naturalization, promotes airport security

7. Besides the departments, what else is included in the federal bureaucracy?

Falling outside the departmental structure are a number of smaller independent agencies that report directly to the president (CIA, Environmental Protection Agency, and the Executive Office of the president). Also included in the federal bureaucracy are a number of independent regulatory agencies whose top officials are appointed by the president and confirmed by the Senate but who operate independently and are not directly subject to presidential control (Securities and Exchange Commission, Federal Trade Commission, and Federal Reserve Board). Finally, the federal bureaucracy includes several governmental corporations who operate somewhat like private businesses (Amtrak, U.S. Postal Service).

8. Why do presidents have only limited power to control the federal bureaucracy?

In theory, the bureaucracy is part of the executive branch and directly under the president's control. However, in reality, the president has only limited control of the federal bureaucracy. Some of the reasons for this are:

- Laws setting up federal agencies provide them with authority to implement certain laws and programs and, unless Congress changes the law, the president is limited in the changes he can make. No president can unilaterally eliminate an agency, its funding, or its programs.

- Much of the government's expertise—whether it's space travel, communicable disease, pollution, forestry, or the response to a disaster—is held by the staff of federal agencies. The president and his appointees rarely have the expertise to challenge the experts and often let them write federal regulations and enforce them with considerable independence.

- Most agencies have powerful clientele groups—special interests that directly benefit from the agency's programs. Presidents are likely to be careful not to interfere too much in the agency's work if a powerful clientele group is likely to become enraged.

- Many federal agencies have strong supporters in Congress. In the final analysis, agencies must please Congress since it provides the funds for federal agencies and programs to operate. Presidents come and go but members of Congress often remain for decades. Federal agencies need to be at least as responsive to Congress as the president and this weakens the president's power over them.

- Finally, it is difficult for the president to truly control the sprawling 2.5-million-member federal bureaucracy. Hundreds of people report directly to the president so presidents must pick and choose where they want to get involved to exert leadership and power.

9. How do the president and Congress control the federal bureaucracy?

The agencies of the federal bureaucracy often operate with considerable independence, but they are subject to controls and limitations. Here are the tools the president and Congress can use to keep the bureaucracy accountable.

- **Presidential appointments** The president appoints key officials of the federal bureaucracy (who must be approved by the Senate) and he has the power to remove these officials from office. Presidential appointees help make sure the federal bureaucracy follows presidential goals and directives. The president relies on these appointees but he cannot keep track of all appointees or instruct them in detail on how to act during their tenure of office. Thus, through his appointments the president can broadly influence the bureaucracy, but not completely control the administration of federal programs and policies.

- **Executive orders** The president can issue executive orders to the federal bureaucracy to control their actions. For example, President Reagan used his executive power to prohibit the use of federal funds by family-planning clinics that offered abortion counseling. Later, President Clinton used his executive power to overturn Reagan's order. In general, the president can issue whatever executive orders to the bureaucracy he wants to as long as they do not violate federal law or the Constitution. The federal bureaucracy must follow presidential directives and this gives the president some control—at least in policy areas in which the president wants to focus—on the actions of federal agencies.

- **OMB** The Office of Management and Budget is a powerful agency within the Executive Office of the President. This office creates the federal budget request, approves federal regulations, and in general makes sure that presidential directives and policies are followed within the federal bureaucracy.

- **Congress's role** Congress has as much power over federal agencies as the president since Congress creates the laws that federal agencies administer, including the laws creating federal agencies themselves. But of even greater significance is that Congress decides each year how much funding each federal agency and program will receive. Thus all federal agencies depend on Congress for their existence, their programs, and their funding. Congress also exerts some control through its oversight function, through which it can conduct investigations and hold public hearings regarding the performance of a federal agency.

Landmark Decisions of the Supreme Court

Myers v. United States (1926) The Supreme Court declared unconstitutional laws that required the president to get approval from the Senate before removing federal officials from office. Thus, the president needs Senate confirmation to appoint key officials to office, but not to remove them. The Court concluded that, since the president is responsible for execution of the laws and he can only execute the laws through subordinates, he must have the power to remove subordinates in whom he lacks confidence. However, the power of the president to remove federal employees extends only to the officials the president nominates or appoints, not to civil service employees who are protected by the civil service system from politically motivated hiring and firing.

U.S. v. Nixon (1974) The Supreme Court unanimously ruled that the president's right of **executive privilege** was limited and could not be used to refuse to provide information about conversations the president has with his advisors when these conversations are pertinent to a criminal trial. As a result, Nixon was forced to turn over tapes of White House conversations related to the Watergate cover-up that also showed his complicity in the crimes his advisors were accused of. He resigned as president shortly thereafter.

Nixon v. Fitzgerald (1982) This decision of the Supreme Court held that the president is immune from civil lawsuits based on official acts performed while president. However, the Court made clear that the president is not immune from criminal charges based on his official acts as president.

Clinton v. Jones (1997) The Supreme Court declared that a sitting president has no immunity—not even temporary immunity until his term of office is over—from civil lawsuits against him for acts committed before he was president that are unrelated to his official duties as president. The Court's decision led to the case of Clinton v. Jones going ahead in U.S. District Court, which eventually led to criminal charges of perjury and obstruction of justice against Clinton and to his impeachment by the House of Representatives (the Senate did not remove him from office).

Clinton v. City of New York (1998) Congress passed the Line-Item Veto Act in 1996, allowing the president to veto specific projects funded in an Appropriations bill passed by Congress. In this case, the Supreme Court ruled that the act was unconstitutional since it gave the president the power to change the "text of duly enacted statutes." The president could veto the entire bill, but not just a part of it.

Topic 4 Review

1. Which of the following is NOT a reason the president often has a hard time controlling the federal bureaucracy?

   A. Most members of the bureaucracy are civil service employees who cannot be hired or fired for political reasons.

   B. The federal bureaucracy is huge and hundreds of people report directly to the president.

   C. Federal agencies ultimately get their money from Congress, not the president.

   D. After the Senate approves a presidential appointee for a key position in government, the president cannot fire the person unless the Senate approves the action.

   E. Federal agencies have their own interests (such as self-preservation and growth) that may conflict with the president's goals and policies.

2. An example of an independent regulatory agency is

   A. the Transportation Security Administration (TSA)
   B. the Federal Trade Commission (FTC)
   C. the Department of Veteran's Affairs
   D. the U.S. Postal Service (USPS)
   E. the FBI

3. In the federal budget, mandatory spending refers to

   A. spending on entitlement programs required by law
   B. earmarks imposed by Congress in the federal budget
   C. spending on interest on the national debt
   D. spending on defense
   E. spending on defense and homeland security

4. Which of the following actions can the president take WITHOUT the approval of the Senate?

    A.   ratify treaties with other nations

    B.   send troops abroad

    C.   appoint U.S. top diplomats, including ambassadors

    D.   appoint judges to U.S. District Court

    E.   select the members of his cabinet

Topic 5: The Supreme Court and the Federal Judiciary

> Before tackling this in-depth review, make sure you've read Big Ideas 3 and 13 and reviewed the key terms relating to the Supreme Court and the federal judiciary.

1. What is the structure of the federal court system?

Article III of the Constitution sets up the Supreme Court and leaves it to Congress to set up a system of inferior federal courts. Congress established U.S. District Courts in 1789 and U.S. Courts of Appeals in 1891.

THE FEDERAL COURT SYSTEM

Court	Jurisdiction	Structure
Supreme Court	**Appellate jurisdiction:** Accepts appeals of decisions made by U.S. Courts of Appeals. **Original jurisdiction:** Serves as trial court for cases between state governments.	The Court consists of one chief justice and eight associate justices—all of whom hear cases before the Court together. It is the court of last appeal in the United States.
Court	Jurisdiction	Structure
U.S. Courts of Appeals	**Appellate jurisdiction only:** U.S. Courts of Appeals accept appeals of cases originally tried in U.S. District Courts. They also accept appeals from state courts if federal law or the U.S. Constitution are involved. U.S. Courts of Appeals conduct no trials; they only review cases to see if the law and the Constitution were correctly interpreted and applied. If a new trial is needed, they remand the case back to the trial court.	Cases are usually heard by a panel of three judges. There are twelve courts of appeals, each serving a region of the United States. One additional U.S. Court of Appeals specializes in cases involving patents and international trade.
U.S. District Courts	**Original jurisdiction:** Cases involving federal law are tried in these courts. This is the only level of the federal court system in which you would find a trial being conducted with juries, witnesses, etc.	Usually only one judge hears a case. There are ninety U.S. District Courts with at least one in each state.

2. How does the Supreme Court decide which cases to hear?

Each year about 10,000 cases come to the Supreme Court; however, it decides to hear only about 100 of these cases. If the Supreme Court decides not to hear a case, the decision of the lower court stands. Four of the nine justices of the Supreme Court must vote in favor of considering an appeal of a case in order for the Supreme Court to grant a writ of certiorari and review the case. The Court seldom takes a routine case, even if it believes a lower court made a mistake; the Court's job is to resolve substantial legal issues, not correct errors. Most cases it decides to hear raise constitutional issues, address issues that are being decided inconsistently by lower courts, or involve rulings that are at odds with a previous Supreme Court decision. The Court usually also agrees to hear cases that the federal government has lost but that the Justice Department wants to appeal.

3. What limitations are there on how an appeals court rules?

In theory at least, Supreme Court justices and the judges of the U.S. Court of Appeals are not free to decide cases based on their own personal opinions. Their decisions are bound by the following restraints:

- **The facts as determined by the trial court** The "facts" of the case are the relevant events and circumstances relating to a legal dispute or crime. The appeals court does not call witnesses and does not consider new evidence, so it must let the findings of the lower court regarding the 'facts" stand. If, however, the appeals court finds that procedures the court used to arrive at the "facts" were flawed and did not comply with federal laws or the Constitution, then it can remand the case back to the trial court for a new trial in which it instructs the lower court to follow a different procedure (which may or may not produce different "facts").
- **Federal law and the Constitution** The appeals court is bound by the wording of applicable federal laws and the Constitution. In reality, however, laws (and the Constitution) are often fairly vague and judges have some freedom in deciding cases based on their own interpretation of the wording in federal laws and the Constitution.

- **Precedent** Federal courts are generally bound to follow precedent (in legal terms this principle is called **stare decisis**). However, in reality judges have some discretion in their evaluation of which previous cases are similar and whether or not a precedent applies to a current case. The Supreme Court, from time to time, overturns precedents. *Brown v. Board of Education* (1954), which declared public school segregation by race unconstitutional, overturned *Plessy v. Ferguson* (1896), which had held it to be constitutional.

4. How are federal judges selected?

The president nominates federal judges, including Supreme Court justices, but they must be confirmed by a majority vote in the Senate. For nominees to the Supreme Court, this confirmation vote has become a highly charged political struggle in which opponents of a president's nominee try to block confirmation, usually through a filibuster, since a filibuster allows a minority to block a vote on confirmation of a justice a majority may approve.

5. What do presidents look for in selecting someone as a nominee for the Supreme Court?

- **Political party and philosophy** presidents almost always nominate someone from their political party and, of course, a president wants someone who shares his political vision and philosophy. However, sometimes presidents are later surprised by the stands their appointees take since, once on the Supreme Court, the political philosophies of justices often shift or evolve over time.

- **Age** Generally, presidents look for a nominee who is young enough to have a long future as a Supreme Court justice. For example, William O. Douglass, appointed by Franklin D. Roosevelt in 1939, continued to be a strong liberal voice on the Court for thirty years after Roosevelt died in 1945.

- **Ability to be confirmed** presidents must also consider the likelihood that a nominee can be confirmed. The backgrounds of nominees are carefully checked to ensure that they are free from scandal or other problems that the opposition could use to establish doubt about their judgment and character. Presidents try to find someone who can gain enough support from senators from the opposition party to prevent a filibuster.

6. What are the main political theories regarding how the Constitution should be interpreted?

- **Originalism theory** This theory, a prominent philosophy of conservatives including Supreme Court Justice Antonin Scalia, holds that judges need to simply determine the original meaning of the words (what they meant at the time they were written) and then apply that meaning to the case at hand. In practice this may be more difficult that it seems because there are many aspects of modern society, such as the Internet, that were simply not dreamed of at the time the Constitution was written.

- **Living Constitution theory** This theory, often advanced by liberals, holds that the writers of the Constitution wanted their words to be flexible enough to be, as a committee of the Constitutional Convention stated, "accommodated to times and events" in the future. This theory, advanced by Supreme Court Justice Stephen Breyer, holds that rather than defining words, judges should be focused on promoting in today's world the kind of government the Constitution was meant to establish.

Landmark Supreme Court Decisions

Marbury v. Madison (1803) Established judicial review. For more description on this decision, see "Landmark Supreme Court Decisions" at the end of Topic 1 (page 92).

Topic 5 Review

1. Of the thousands of cases appealed to the Supreme Court, who determines which ones the Supreme Court will hear?

    A.   the justices themselves by unanimous consent

    B.   the justices themselves by a vote in which at least four of the nine justices vote to hear the case

    C.   the Solicitor General of the United States decides which cases should go to the Supreme Court

    D.   the U. S. Courts of Appeal decide which cases should go to the Supreme Court

    E.   the Attorney General

2. Federal courts which serve mainly as appellate courts are

    A.   U.S. District Courts only

    B.   U.S. Courts of Appeal only

    C.   the Supreme Court and the U.S. Courts of Appeal only

    D.   U.S. District Courts, U.S. Courts of Appeal, and the Supreme Court

    E.   the Supreme Court only

3. *Stare decisis* is

   A.   the principle that the Supreme Court is the highest court of appeal

   B.   the principle that judges should show restraint and leave public policy making to the legislative and executive branches of government

   C.   the principle that if the Supreme Court decides not to hear a case, the decision of the lower court stands

   D.   the principle that judges should serve life terms to free them from political pressures

   E.   the principle that courts should follow precedent in making legal decisions in cases

4. Cases that involve civil law are

   A.   cases regarding possible violations of civil rights law

   B.   cases involving state laws only

   C.   disputes between private parties in which there is no criminal prosecution by a government

   D.   criminal prosecutions by the government

   E.   cases involving civilians rather than military law and military courts

Topic 6: Civil Liberties

Before tackling this in-depth review, make sure you've read
Big Ideas 5, 6, and 7 and reviewed the key terms relating
to civil liberties.

1. Are there limits on the civil liberties guaranteed by the Bill of Rights?

None of the rights in the Bill of Rights are absolute. In practice, the rights of one person may conflict with the rights of another. Or there may be an overriding government interest that requires a right to be limited or curtailed. Freedom of speech is among the most basic rights in a democracy and the Supreme Court has zealously defended it, often taking unpopular positions to uphold the rights of individuals to speak in ways that the majority finds repugnant. However, even freedom of speech has limits. The Supreme Court has held that free speech is not okay if it is obscene, slanders another person, or has a high probability of inciting "imminent lawless action." The Court has also upheld restrictions on free speech when justified by the government's overwhelming need to protect national security. In short, exactly what the limits are on a person's rights is a subject constantly being reviewed by the courts.

2. If the rights are spelled out in the Bill of Rights, why is there so much disagreement on what they are?

The language in the Bill of Rights is general and many of the terms, such as "unreasonable" and "cruel and unusual," are open to interpretation. In fact, the Second Amendment leaves open to interpretation whether the right to bear arms is really a right at all. Until *District of Columbia v. Heller* (2008), the courts had held that the right was linked to service in a militia and there was no right to bear arms independent of service in a militia. Nevertheless, most people agree on the rights when stated in general terms; the disagreement comes when applying the language in the Bill of Rights to real-life situations. Then there is usually strong disagreement among justices on the Supreme Court regarding what the language of the Bill of Rights means and how the language should be applied to actual situations.

3. What are the fundamental civil liberties protected by the Bill of Rights?

The chart below summarizes the most important rights guaranteed by the Constitution; most of these are in the Bill of Rights (first ten amendments to the Constitution).

IMPORTANT CIVIL LIBERTIES

Right	Where Stated	Landmark Court Cases (see descriptions at the end of this chapter)
Freedom of expression Includes: Freedom of speech, freedom of the press, and freedom to peacefully protest	First Amendment	*Brandenberg v. Ohio* *Texas v. Johnson* *Schenk v. United States* *Holder v. Humanitarian Law Project* *New York Times Company v. United States*

Freedom of religion Includes free-exercise clause and establishment clause	First Amendment	*Wisconsin v. Yoder* *Engle v. Vitale* *Edwards v. Aguillard* *Tilton v. Richardson* *Zelman v. Simmons-Harris*
Right to bear arms	Second Amendment	*District of Columbia v. Heller*
Protection from unreasonable searches and seizures	Fourth Amendment	*Mapp v. Ohio*
Rights of the accused Includes: right to due process of law, right to an attorney, right to confront witnesses against you, the right to remain silent, the right to a speedy trial, right to trial by an impartial jury, prohibition of double jeopardy	Fifth and Sixth Amendments	*Gideon v. Wainright* *Miranda v. Arizona*
Restrictions on eminent domain	Fifth and Sixth Amendments	*Kelso v. City of New London*
Prohibition of cruel and unusual punishment	Eighth Amendment	*Gregg v. Georgia* *Atkins v. Virginia* *Roper v. Simmons*
Right to privacy	Implied in Bill of Rights	*Griswold v. Connecticut* *Roe v. Wade* *Lawrence v. Texas*

4. What is the relationship of the Fourteenth Amendment to the Bill of Rights?

The Fourteenth Amendment was passed after the Civil War to prevent states from denying the rights of citizens to former slaves. The due process clause of the Fourteenth Amendment (1868) does not add any rights to the Bill of Rights; however, the Supreme Court has used this clause to apply the Bill of Rights to state governments, rather than just to the federal government. In *Gitlow v. New York* (1925), the Court ruled that state governments could not restrict the rights of freedom of speech and the press contained in the First Amendment. Subsequent decisions have added most other civil liberties in the Bill of Rights to those rights that state governments must also respect. As a result of the decision in *Gitlow v. New York*, cases involving the abridgement of civil liberties by state government can now be taken to federal courts for consideration.

5. What rights are guaranteed by the Constitution other than those in the Bill of Rights?

The Bill of Rights is a listing of the most important civil liberties guaranteed to the American people. However, other parts of the U.S. Constitution also contain basic rights.

- **Prohibition of bills of attainder** Article I prohibits legislative acts declaring a person or group of persons guilty of a crime and punishing them without benefit of a trial. This applies to federal and state governments.

- **Writ of habeas corpus** Article I protects the right of someone convicted of a crime to file a legal action of challenging the conviction by asking a court to review the record of the trial to determine if the law was correctly interpreted and applied.

- **Prohibition of ex post facto laws** Articles I prohibits Congress and the state legislatures from passing laws making an action a crime retroactively, although it wasn't a crime when the action took place.

Landmark Supreme Court Decisions

Brandenberg v. Ohio (1969) In its decision the Court held that the First Amendment protected a speech given at a Ku Klux Klan rally calling for the use of illegal force. In this case the Court established the "imminent lawless action" test, saying that unless there was the threat of imminent lawless action, the government could not prohibit speech, even if it advocated taking unlawful action.

Texas v. Johnson (1989) The Supreme Court ruled that flag burning was a form of **symbolic free speech** protected by the First Amendment. It declared a Texas law banning flag burning to be unconstitutional.

Schenck v. United States (1919) The Supreme Court's decision declared that the Espionage Act of 1917, which restricted speech critical of the government's war effort during World War I, was constitutional. The Court upheld the conviction of a draft resister who was handing out anti-draft pamphlets to soldiers. The Court's decision established the "clear and present danger" test; if free speech could result in a danger to national security in wartime, the Court ruled that certain types of speech could be prohibited.

Holder v. Humanitarian Law Project (2010) The Humanitarian Law Project, a nonprofit group, wanted to help a Turkish group on the U.S. government's terrorist list develop legal, nonviolent means of promoting their cause. It challenged the Patriot Act, which made it a crime to help a terrorist group in any way, claiming that it infringed on freedom of speech. The Supreme Court decision upheld the Patriot Act saying that Congress could prohibit aid to terrorists and define what "aid" meant, thus ending the Humanitarian Law Project's effort to get terrorist groups to replace terrorism with legal activities.

New York Times Company v. United States (1971) In this case the Court ruled that the government could not stop the *New York Times* from publishing the Pentagon Papers (secret government documents revealing top officials had deceived the public regarding the Vietnam War). Although the *Times* could be held accountable for violation of a law after publication, the Court ruled that a system of **"prior restraint"** on the press amounted to censorship and is unconstitutional.

Engle v. Vitale (1962) The Supreme Court ruled that the recitation of prayers written by the government in public schools was a violation of the establishment clause of the First Amendment and thus unconstitutional. In 1963 it declared that Bible-reading in public schools was also a violation of the establishment clause (*School District of Abington Township v. Schempp*).

Edwards v. Aguillard (1987) The Supreme Court ruled that a Louisiana law requiring public schools to teach "creation science" advances religion and thereby violates the establishment clause of the First Amendment. The Court said that the purpose of the law was to restructure the science curriculum to conform with a particular religious viewpoint.

Tilton v. Richardson (1971) The Court upheld federal aid to church-related private colleges to construct academic buildings but invalidated a provision of the law that would have allowed the buildings to be used for religious purposes after 20 years. The Court held that such aid promoted the government's interest in education and did not cause an excessive entanglement between church and state.

Zelman v. Simmons-Harris (2002) The Court upheld an Ohio law that provided government-funded school vouchers that could be used at private schools—including religious schools—as well as public schools. Since the program provided vouchers to individuals (rather than parochial schools) and parents had a choice of which school their children would attend, the Court held that the vouchers did not involve excessive government "entanglement with religion."

Wisconsin v. Yoder (1972) The Supreme Court unanimously voided the conviction of Amish parents who had refused to send their children to school beyond eighth grade on religious grounds. It declared the state's interest in providing an education did not override the right of parents to the free exercise of their religion.

District of Columbia v. Heller (2008) Previously, the Supreme Court had held that, due to the wording of the Second Amendment, the right to bear arms was connected to service in a state militia. In *District of Columbia v. Heller* (2008), however, the Court reversed itself and declared a constitutional right to gun ownership independent of being a member of a state militia.

Mapp v. Ohio (1961) The Supreme Court ruled that evidence obtained in violation of the Fourth Amendment's prohibition of unreasonable searches and seizures must be excluded from use at state as well as federal trials. The exclusionary rule was later applied to other violations of rights by police (see *Miranda v. Arizona* below).

Gideon v. Wainright (1963) The Supreme Court ruled that states had to provide an attorney in felony cases for defendants unable to afford one on their own. The case is based on the Sixth Amendment, which guarantees that the accused shall have the "Assistance of Counsel for his defence."

Miranda v. Arizona (1966) The Supreme Court extended the protection of the self-incrimination clause of the Fifth Amendment by requiring police to inform persons in custody prior to questioning of their rights to remain silent and to have an attorney. The exclusionary rule requires that evidence obtained from a suspect not told these rights is not admissible in court, although the Supreme Court since 1966 has carved out exceptions to this rule.

Kelso v. City of New London (2005) The Supreme Court upheld the power of eminent domain of the New London to take private property even though the property was to be resold by the city to a private developer rather than retained by the city for public use. The Court held the Constitution imposed no restrictions on eminent domain except that for just compensation and due process of law contained in the Fifth and Sixth Amendments.

Gregg v. Georgia (1976) The Court ruled that the death penalty was not unconstitutional but that it couldn't be administered in a mandatory way. In other words, the sentencing judge and jury had to take into account the character of the offender and the circumstances of the particular case.

Atkins v. Virginia (2002) The court ruled that the execution of mentally retarded felons violates the Eighth Amendment ban on cruel and unusual punishment.

Roper v. Simmons (2005) The Court ruled that convicts who committed their crimes before they reached 18 could not be executed because this constitutes cruel and unusual punishment when applied to minors.

Griswold v. Connecticut (1965) Although no individual right to privacy is specifically stated in the Bill of Rights, the Supreme Court has determined that the freedoms in the Bill of Rights imply an underlying right to privacy. The right to privacy was established in *Griswold v. Connecticut* (1965), which declared unconstitutional a state law prohibiting the use of birth control devices even by married couples.

Roe v. Wade (1973) The Supreme Court determined that the right to privacy is "broad enough to encompass a woman's decision on whether or not to terminate a pregnancy." Since this decision, the Court has upheld state laws restricting abortion procedures.

Lawrence v. Texas (2003) The Court has also applied the right to privacy to sexual relations between consenting adults; in *Lawrence v. Texas* (2003) it ruled that states could not criminalize private consensual sex between adults of the same sex, striking down sodomy laws in the thirteen states that still had them. This decision overturned the Court's decision in *Bowers v. Hardwick* (1986).

Topic 6 Review

1. In what amendment in the Constitution are the rights of the accused guaranteed, including the right to an attorney, the right to be told the charges against you, and the right to remain silent?

   A. the First Amendment
   B. the Second Amendment
   C. the Fourth Amendment
   D. the Fifth and Sixth Amendments
   E. the rights listed are not explicitly stated in the Constitution but were established in the Supreme Court's decision in *Miranda v. Arizona* (1966).

2. In 1965, the Supreme Court first recognized a right to privacy implied—but not explicitly stated—in the Bill of Rights in its decision in

   A. *Roe v. Wade*
   B. *Lawrence v. Texas*
   C. *Griswold v. Connecticut*
   D. *Gitlow v. New York*
   E. *Wisconsin v. Yoder*

3. In *District of Columbia v. Heller* (2008), the Supreme Court ruled that the Second Amendment's right to bear arms

   A. gives people the right to carry guns in public
   B. prohibits government from restricting the purchase of firearms
   C. makes it unconstitutional for the government to require gun registration
   D. gives individuals a right to gun ownership that is independent of service in a state militia
   E. is restricted to service in a state militia

4. What is the "excessive entanglement with religion" test?

    A.   a legal principle the Supreme Court has developed to enforce a complete separation of church and state

    B.   a test designed to ensure that nominees to the Supreme Court are unbiased

    C.   a guideline for evaluating and accrediting parochial schools

    D.   a guideline established by the Supreme Court to determine if a government activity violates the free exercise clause of the First Amendment

    E.   a guideline established by the Supreme Court to determine if a government activity violates the establishment clause of the First Amendment

Topic 7: The Struggle for Equal Rights

> Before tackling this in-depth review, make sure you've read Big Idea 8 and reviewed the key terms relating to the struggle for equal rights.

1. What were the landmark achievements of the Civil Rights Movement?

The Civil Rights Movement in the 1950s and 1960s achieved, for the most part, its goal of removing legal barriers to equality between blacks and whites. These achievements are shown in the chart included with Big Idea 8, "Equal Rights."

2. What have been the landmark achievements of the women's rights movement?

At the time the Constitution was written, the United States political system discounted women, forbidding them from voting, holding public office, or serving on juries. Upon marriage, a woman lost her identity as an individual and came under her husband's control. The first women's rights convention in the United States was held in 1848 in Seneca Falls, New York, after women were barred from the main floor of an antislavery convention. Selected achievements of the women's rights movement are summarized in the chart below:

LANDMARK ACHIEVEMENTS OF WOMEN'S RIGHTS MOVEMENT

Description	Year	Type of Action	Significance
Nineteenth Amendment	1920	constitutional amendment	Gave women the right to vote in state and federal elections
Reed v. Reed	1971	Supreme Court decision	Applied the Fourteenth Amendment's equal protection clause to eliminate preferential treatment of males over females in state laws. (See description of case below.)
Equal Employment Opportunity Act	1972	federal law	Prohibited discrimination by gender in hiring, firing, promotions, working conditions, and pay
Title IX	1972	federal law	Required education systems receiving federal grants to give male and female students an equal opportunity to participate in sports activities
Equal Credit Opportunity Act	1974	federal law	Prohibited discrimination against women seeking credit from banks, finance agencies, or the government
Family Leave Act	1993	federal law	Required large employers to provide job-protected unpaid leave to their employees to care for a sick family member or new child

3. What is affirmative action and is it constitutional?

Affirmative action refers to government programs that grant preferences to minorities in order to correct discrimination and increase the number of minorities enrolled in higher education or working in certain trades/professions. However, affirmative action has been considered "reverse discrimination" by whites who found themselves excluded as a result of the preferences given minorities. In *University of California Regents v. Bakke* (1978), the Supreme Court declared the use of racial quotas to promote minority enrollment in the University of California to be a violation of the equal protection clause of the Fourteenth Amendment, while not making a ruling on other methods of affirmative action. Gradually, the Supreme Court issued decisions that restricted government affirmative action programs, finally declaring them to be a violation of the equal protection clause. However, in *Grutter v. Bollinger* (2003), the Court ruled that race could be used as one factor in college admissions at a state university (along with factors such as ethnic identity, gender, etc.) to ensure the diversity conducive to quality education. But, affirmative action, as a policy to achieve better racial balance or redress past discrimination, was dead.

4. How have the Supreme Court's views on ending school desegregation evolved?

In *Brown v. Board of Education*, the Supreme Court declared **de jure school segregation** by race (required by law) unconstitutional. **De facto school segregation** (caused not by law but by residential patterns) proved more difficult. In *Swan v. Charlotte-Mecklenburg County Board of Education* (1971), the court required busing to integrate schools where residential patterns, rather than segregation laws, produced school segregation. "Forced" busing proved to be very unpopular politically and led to a widespread perception that the Court had overstepped its role and become too involved in national policy formulation. Court-ordered busing in many cities contributed to white flight to private schools and to the suburbs, making it harder than ever to achieve racial balance and convince taxpayers to fund public schools adequately. The Supreme Court gradually backed away from requiring busing to achieve racial balance and in Seattle and Louisville in 2007 switched positions and declared that race could not be a factor in assigning students to schools, effectively ending efforts to achieve racial balance where segregation is caused by residential patterns.

5. What have been the achievements of the struggle by the GLBT community for equal rights?

The demand for equal rights by the GLBT (gay, lesbian, bisexual, and transgendered) community is one of the most controversial political issues in the United States today. At the time of publication of this book, the GLBT movement had achieved the right to marry in several states and the District of Columbia and to civil unions in several more states. *Lawrence v. Bowers* (2003) had decriminalized consensual sex between same-sex adults and *Romer v. Evans* (1996) had invalidated a state's attempt to restrict GLBT rights (see descriptions of these cases below). However, GLBT groups still sought marriage rights in the remaining states, protections in federal law from discrimination, the right to serve openly in the U.S. military, and repeal of the Defense of Marriage Act.

Landmark Supreme Court Decisions

Scott v. Sandford (1857) Commonly known as the **Dred Scott Decision**. Dred Scott, a slave, sued for his freedom after his owner took him into the Wisconsin territory where slavery was outlawed. The Supreme Court ruled that Scott remained a slave because he was property and the Constitution prevented the taking of property without due process of law. The decision further held that, as property, slaves were not citizens and could not sue in the courts. The decision declared that Congress could not prohibit slavery in federal territories since it could not deprive a person of their property without due process, thus invalidating the Missouri Compromise and opening the entire West to slavery. The decision outraged the North and helped lead to the Civil War. After the war, the Dred Scott Decision was overturned by the Fourteenth Amendment (1868), which declared that slaves were citizens and entitled to the equal protection of the law by state governments.

Brown v. Board of Education of Topeka (1954) The Supreme Court declared that separate schools for African Americans were inherently unequal and a violation of the equal protection clause of the Fourteenth Amendment. This decision overturned **Plessy v. Ferguson** (1896), which had allowed separate facilities for African Americans. One of the most important decisions of the Court in the twentieth century, *Brown v. Board of Education* helped give rise to the Civil Rights Movement and years of struggle to end racial segregation, not only in education but in all types of public facilities.

University of California Regents v. Bakke (1978) Alan Bakke, a white person, was denied admission to medical school because of a race-based quota system intended to increase the number of African Americans in the overwhelmingly white institution. Such preferential treatment was known as affirmative action and was designed to counter years of discrimination. Without invalidating the principle of affirmative action, the Supreme Court ruled that a quota system based solely on race was unconstitutional and violated the "equal protection of the law" that all citizens are entitled to.

Grutter v. Bollinger (2003) In this decision, the Court ruled that race could be used as one factor in college admissions (along with factors such as ethnic identity, gender, etc.) to ensure the diversity conducive to quality education. However, granting special preferences on the basis of race to either redress past discrimination or achieve racial balance (affirmative action programs) was an unconstitutional violation of the Fourteenth Amendment's "equal protection of the laws" clause.

Swann v. Charlotte-Mecklenburg County Board of Education (1971) The Supreme Court required busing of children to integrate schools that were segregated because of racially separate neighborhoods. This ruling attempted to end **de facto** school segregation (segregation caused by social, economic, and cultural factors); *Brown v. Board of Education* only addressed **de jure** segregation (segregation caused by law).

Loving v. Virginia (1967) The Supreme Court overturned a Virginia law that prohibited interracial marriage on the grounds that this violated the equal protection clause of the Fourteenth Amendment. Previously in *Alabama v. Pace* (1883), the Court had found that laws against interracial sex and marriage did not violate the equal protection clause as long as both white and black partners were punished equally.

Reed v. Reed (1971) Based on the Fourteenth Amendment's equal protection clause, the Court's decision eliminated preferences enjoyed by males over females in state laws. After the death of their son, the Reeds (who were divorced) each sought to be named administrator of their son's estate. Idaho law required that males be granted preference over women for this position. The Court overturned the Idaho law and applied the equal protection clause to females, ruling that state laws may not grant preferences based on gender.

Romer v. Evans (1996) The Court declared unconstitutional an amendment to the Colorado state constitution that prohibited local governments from passing local ordinances protecting equal rights of GLBT persons. It ruled that the amendment denied one class of people the equal protection of law by prohibiting them from advancing their goals through the political process. The Court's decision allowed anti-discrimination measures to stand in Denver, Boulder, and Aspen and allowed GLBT people to continue to participate in the political process to get similar laws passed in other cities.

Korematsu v. U.S. (1944) This case challenged a presidential executive order that ordered Japanese Americans living on the West Coast—many of whom were U.S. citizens—into internment camps during World War II. The Supreme Court held that the need to protect the national security of the United States outweighed the individual rights of Fred Korematsu to due process of law before being deprived of liberty. It demonstrates the reluctance of the courts to interfere with military policies in time of war. Although this decision has not been overturned, it has been widely acknowledged that the internment of Japanese Americans was based on racism, not national security. In 1980 Congress passed a law under which reparations were paid to Japanese Americans who were interned and in 1998 Fred Korematsu was a recipient of the Presidential Medal of Freedom.

Topic 7 Review

1. The goal of the women's suffrage movement was

    A. getting equality for women
    B. obtaining the right to vote for women
    C. prohibiting the sale and manufacture of alcoholic beverages
    D. reducing the number of women suffering from mistreatment by males
    E. getting women elected to public office

2. In *University of California Regents v. Bakke* (1978), the Supreme Court ruled that

    A. The University of California must institute a quota system in order to eliminate racial segregation in its schools.
    B. The University of California could use a quota system to create schools that reflected the racial balance of the state.
    C. Racial quotas could not be used to provide racial balance in state universities.
    D. All affirmative action programs giving preferences to people solely on the basis of race were unconstitutional.
    E. The University of California must offer remedial help to minority students who did not get a good high school education.

3. Poll taxes and literacy tests were widely used throughout the South to reduce voter turnout among African Americans until they were finally eliminated by

    A.   the repeal of Jim Crow Laws in each state in the 1960s and 1970s

    B.   the Supreme Court's decision in *Loving v. Virginia* (1967)

    C.   the ratification of the Twenty-Fourth Amendment (1964) and the passage of the Voting Rights Act of 1965

    D.   the passage of the Civil Rights Act of 1964

    E.   an executive order prohibiting racial segregation was issued by President John F. Kennedy

4. In *Reed v. Reed* (1971), the Supreme Court declared unconstitutional

    A.   preferences granted males over females in civil law

    B.   discrimination on the basis of sexual orientation

    C.   state laws prohibiting interracial marriage

    D.   racial segregation in restaurants, stores, hotels, and other public accommodations

    E.   racial quotas designed to achieve balance in hiring and promoting governmental employees

Topic 8: Political Parties and Elections

Before tackling this in-depth review, make sure you've read Big Ideas 14, 15, and 16 and reviewed the key terms relating to political parties and elections.

1. What three meanings are given to the term "political party" in American politics?

- **Party membership** *Political party* can mean the people who identify themselves as members of a political party. There is no official membership list; people are considered members of a political party if they say they are.
- **Party organization** The term can also be used to refer to the party's organized structure and the people who are actively engaged in party activities.
- **Party in government** Finally, the term can be used to mean the people who have been elected to official positions in government under a party's name.

2. What common types of party systems are found in modern democracies?

- **Two-party systems** Two parties representing large coalitions of interests compete with each other for power. The U.S. political system has been a two-party system composed of Democratic and Republican parties since the Civil War. In a two-party system each political party attempts to put together the largest coalition of interests to create a majority party—a reality that often leads political parties to move toward the center of the left-right political spectrum. Two-party systems are usually characterized by single-member legislative districts (contrast with multiparty systems below).

- **Multiparty systems** Multiparty systems exist where representation is based not on the winner in a specific geographic district (single-member district), but on the share of the nationwide popular vote a party gets. In multiparty systems, a coalition of political parties must often be formed to create a government with the required legislative majority. Most of the world's modern democracies are multiparty systems.

3. What roles do political parties play in the American political system?

The overriding goal of political parties is to win elections. To accomplish that end they do all the following:

- **Recruit candidates** Parties try to find candidates who they think can win election and then persuade them to run. An ideal candidate is one who is well known and well liked by the electorate, who can raise the money needed (or, increasingly, just have it themselves), who comes across well on television, among other factors. Often parties recruit politicians who've been in some other elective office, but other times they have recruited sports heroes, military heroes, TV personalities, movie stars, and even an astronaut.

- **Nominate candidates** Through political party primaries (or, for president, a national party convention), political parties choose the one candidate for each office who will run under the party's name and with its support.

- **Support candidates** Once officially selected, the party supports its candidate with fundraising and efforts to get the people who are usually supportive of its candidate to vote. Get-out-the-vote efforts are particularly important since candidates win not by having the greatest popular support, but by getting the most voters that support them to the polls.

- **Organize the government** Once elected, party members band together with other party members to either form the government (if a majority) or form the opposition. The parties themselves have little influence on elected officials once they are elected, but elected officials usually find it necessary to band together with other elected party members to maximize their political clout. Since most officials want to be reelected, they try to govern in a way that will help them win the next election.

4. With which parties do different groups of people in the United States generally identify?

Political parties must build large coalitions if they are to gain power in Congress or win the presidency. For the most part, the coalitions carry over from election to election. A **political realignment** takes place when there is a significant shift in the coalitions each political party represents. Franklin D. Roosevelt's New Deal produced a political realignment that defined the Democratic and Republican parties for decades. In the 1960s and 1970s the strong support of the national Democratic Party for the Civil Rights Movement produced a political realignment that turned the South from solidly Democratic to strongly Republican.

- **Coalition supporting the Republican Party** The Republican Party dominates in the South and Great Plains regions. Groups that are most likely to vote Republican are whites, males, business owners, farmers, middle-aged voters, and households in which no one is a labor union member.

- **Coalition supporting the Democratic Party** The Democratic Party dominates in the Northeast and West Coast regions. Groups most likely to vote Democratic are African Americans, Hispanics, Jews, women, households in which someone is a labor union member, and young voters. The average household income for Democratic voters is much lower than for Republican voters.

5. What about "third" parties (minor parties) in a two-party system?

Although the same two parties—Democratic and Republican—have dominated U.S. elections for the 150 years since the Civil War, many third parties have also been formed during this time. The types of third parties are:

- **Ideological parties** Parties like the Green Party, Libertarian Party, and Socialist Worker Party are often on the ballot in addition to the slates of candidates offered by the two major parties. Their supporters comprise a tiny percentage of the electorate and these parties don't play much of a role in American government. However, in rare cases they can influence elections; in 2000 the 3 percent of the national vote garnered by Green Party candidate Ralph Nader was credited by some with electing George W. Bush by siphoning liberal voters away from Al Gore.

- **Splinter parties** Occasionally, a deep political disagreement may create a splinter party that breaks off from the main party to form a third party. This is most likely to occur when the country is deeply divided and when a strong personality with a devoted group of followers does not win the party nomination. In 1912, the Republican Party split between backers of President William Howard Taft and of former President Theodore Roosevelt, allowing the Democratic nominee, Woodrow Wilson, to be elected. Theodore Roosevelt's splinter "Bull Moose" Party won 27 percent of the popular vote—the largest share ever won by a third party in the United States. In 1948, southern delegates walked out of the Democratic national convention and nominated Senator Strom Thurmond as the presidential nominee of the splinter States' Rights Party, which won thirty-nine electoral votes, but did not stop Democratic nominee Harry Truman from winning the presidency.

- **Single-issue parties** Other third parties have formed around a single issue about which some people feel very strongly but which the two main parties don't want to address for a variety of reasons. Examples have been the Greenback Party (which wanted the U.S. currency to be based on paper money, not gold or silver), the Prohibition Party (which wanted the sale and manufacture of alcohol made illegal), and the Right to Life Party (which wants abortion made illegal). Ironically, single-issue parties, if they are relatively successful, don't last long because their position is adopted by a major party, taking the steam out of the third party.

6. How are political parties structured?

Both Republican and Democratic parties have similar organizational structures at the national, state, and local levels.

- **National party convention** Held every four years to select the party's nominee for president. Delegates to the convention are chosen through a combination of primary elections, local party caucuses, and state conventions, depending on the laws of each state.

- **National committee** A national committee composed of members from each state heads the national party organization. National committee members are chosen by state party committees, which head the party structure at the state level.

- **National party chairperson** Elected by the national committee, this person speaks for the party and manages the party's headquarters in Washington, DC. By tradition the president is the leader of his political party and selects the national party chairperson.

7. Why is the power of political parties declining?

A hundred years ago, party organizations enjoyed almost complete control of nominations and often elections themselves. Today they are not as important and their power continues to decline. Some reasons for the decline are:

- **Decline of patronage systems** Winning parties used to be able to reward their most active members with jobs in government. But patronage systems (also called "spoils systems") have now been replaced, for the most part, with merit-based civil service systems. The powerful **party machines** of a hundred years ago that ran cities and controlled access to government jobs no longer exist except in a few cities like Chicago, where remnants of the old party machine still exist.

- **Loss of party control over the nominations process** A hundred years ago party leaders (often called "party bosses") selected the party's candidates. Today that is almost completely done through primary elections that give this power to the voters. Nonpartisan blanket primaries go even farther, virtually removing political parties from the candidate selection process.

- **Changes in campaign funding and support** Candidates used to rely on political parties for campaign financing and support. Today candidates raise most of the money for their campaigns themselves and have their own campaign organizations independent of their political party.

- **Decline in party identification** Growing numbers of people identify themselves as independents (no party affiliation). Increasingly people vote for the candidate, not the political party. Independents have been elected to the Senate (in 2010 there were two senators with no party membership) and even run for president (H. Ross Perot won 19 percent of the popular vote as an independent in 1992).

8. Who makes the rules for federal elections?

The Constitution sets the nationwide date for the general election for federal offices (president, senator, and U.S. representative). Amendments to the Constitution have defined who is eligible to vote; the Fifteenth Amendment (1870) prohibits states from restricting the right to vote based on race, the Nineteenth Amendment (1920) does the same based on gender, and the Twenty-sixth Amendment (1971) prohibits states from restricting the right to vote to individuals eighteen and older on the basis of age. However beyond that, elections—even federal elections—are governed by state laws. Thus, procedures for registering to vote, qualifying to run, becoming a party's candidate, and for voting itself differ greatly from state to state.

9. What is the importance of voter turnout?

Elections are often won not on the basis of which candidate has the most support among the people, but on the basis of which candidate is most effective in getting his/her supporters to go to the polls and vote. Voter turnout is generally lower among groups that have traditionally supported the Democratic Party, so the Democrats are usually much more supportive of laws to relax voting regulations and make voter registration and voting itself easier. Turnout is consistently lower in midterm elections than in elections in which the president is being elected, so Republicans often have an edge over Democrats in midterm elections.

10. What efforts have states made to increase voter turnout?

Voter turnout in the United States is low compared to most other Western democracies. Some states have attempted to increase turnout by changing voter registration and the process of voting itself. Among the actions being tried in some states are the abolition of voter registration deadlines (allowing people to register as late as Election Day itself), voting by mail, and extension of the voting period to cover more than one day. All states have adopted "motor voter" laws making it easy for people to register to vote at the same time and place they renew their drivers licenses; this is the result of Congress making this action by state governments a prerequisite to obtaining federal highway grants.

11. What have been the effects of campaign finance reform?

Enormous amounts of money are needed to run a campaign for Congress. Money is needed mainly for television advertising but also for political consultants, public opinion polling, and get-out-the-vote efforts. The need for money means that individuals, corporations, and interest groups with money can gain considerable influence over senators and representatives, giving them the more power in influencing these leaders than the public that actually elects them. To limit the influence of money on candidates, campaign reform laws have been passed limiting the amount of money individuals, interest groups, corporations, and even political parties can give to any one candidate. In theory at least, candidates are thus encouraged to raise a little money from a lot of people, rather than relying on just a few contributors with big pockets. However, Supreme Court decisions in *Buckley v. Valeo* (1976) and *Citizens United v. Federal Elections Commission* (2010) declared some of the limitations on campaign contributions and campaign-related spending to be unconstitutional (see case descriptions below). In reality, big money still has a big influence in the electoral process.

Landmark Supreme Court Decisions

Buckley v. Valeo (1976) In 1974, Congress passed, over President Gerald Ford's veto, the first comprehensive effort by the federal government to regulate campaign contributions and spending. In *Buckley v. Valeo* the Supreme Court upheld some of these provisions, including the limitations on campaign contributions to any one candidate and the requirement for the public disclosure of campaign contributions and spending. However, other provisions, including the limitation on how much a candidate could spend on his/her own campaign and the limitation on the amounts independent groups could spend on an election, were a violation of their freedom of speech and therefore unconstitutional. Those opposed to the decision argued that the Court was letting a few people of wealth drown out the free speech of average citizens.

Citizens United v. Federal Elections Commission (2010) In 2002, Congress passed further campaign spending restrictions, known as the McCain-Feingold Act, which banned for-profit and not-for-profit corporations and labor unions from spending their general funds for their own ads supporting or opposing the election of a candidate for federal office. In *Citizens United*, the Supreme Court overturned this provision as a violation of freedom of speech, allowing corporations and labor unions to spend unlimited amounts of money for their own ads in support or opposition to a particular candidate.

Topic 8 Review

1. Which of the following statements best describes an open primary election?

    A. an election that is open only to voters registered as party members, who must vote for candidates on the ballot of the party with which they are registered

    B. an election that is open to all voters regardless of party registration, who vote on one large ballot that contains the all candidates for all offices

    C. an election that is open to all voters, who can select which party's primary election ballot they want to use to vote

    D. an election that is open to all voters, who may vote on the primary election ballots of different political parties in the same election

    E. an election, such as a presidential preference primary, that is open to candidates from all states, rather than just candidates living in the state

2. Which of the following is NOT a reason the power of political parties in the American political system is in decline?

    A. Patronage systems that used to reward the winning political party's supporters with government jobs have been replaced by civil service systems.

    B. Candidates now raise most of the own campaign funds and run their own campaigns often with little support from a political party.

    C. Primary elections have replaced party leaders in selecting a party's candidates so that now political parties have little control over who their candidates are.

    D. Increasing numbers of voters identify themselves as "independents" and are less likely to identify with a political party.

    E. Third parties have become more common, taking away from the power of the two dominant political parties.

3. A result of the system used in the Electoral College in which the candidate with the most votes gets all of the state's electoral votes is that presidential candidates

   A.   try to increase their vote in states in which they already have strong support

   B.   try to build support in the states in which they have the least support

   C.   focus only on the largest states such as New York, California, and Texas

   D.   focus only on a few swing states—especially large states—in which polls indicate the election is close

   E.   focus on all states equally since all states cast electoral votes

4. Which one of the following groups of voters is most likely to vote for a Democrat?

   A.   African Americans, business owners, males

   B.   people under 30, whites, business owners

   C.   African Americans, labor union members, people under age 30

   D.   whites, males, labor union members

   E.   African Americans, business owners, people under age 30

Topic 9: Interest Groups

Before tackling this in-depth review, make sure you've read Big Idea 17 and reviewed the key terms relating to interest groups.

1. What types of interest groups are there?

There are many different types of interest groups and no widely accepted way to divide them into categories. However, categories are useful in explaining the wide range of interest groups, and AP test takers should be aware of different types of interest groups. One way of categorizing interest groups is provided here:

- **Economic interest groups** Economic interest groups are ones whose main goal is to get economic benefits for their members. This category includes most interest groups and encompasses individual corporations (Boeing, General Motors), business groups (Association of Wheat Growers, National Association of Manufacturers), professional organizations (National Education Association, American Medical Association), and labor unions (AFL-CIO, International Brotherhood of Teamsters).

- **Noneconomic interest groups** (also called citizen's groups) Interest groups that are not primarily concerned with enriching themselves include:
  - **Single-issue interest groups** Many interest groups are organized around a specific cause, such as Mothers Against Drunk Driving, the Environmental Defense Fund, the National Rifle Association, and the Human Rights Campaign (equal rights for GLBT persons).
  - **Ideological interest groups** Ideological groups get involved in a broad array of issues in order to promote a particular political philosophy. The leading conservative interest group is the American Conservative Union; on the liberal side are Americans for Democratic Action and MoveOn.org.
  - **Interest groups representing a particular group** An example of this type of group is the American Association of Retired Persons (AARP). Some issues the group may get involved in are economic (for example, Social Security), but other issues are not (age discrimination). The American Legion and the American Association of People with Disabilities are other examples of this type of group.
  - **Public interest groups** These groups are generally organized to promote the public interest rather than a personal interest. Examples include Common Cause (which has focused on government ethics and accountability, especially campaign finance reform) and the League of Women Voters (which works to educate the public about candidates and issues).
  - **Governmental interest groups** While virtually all interest groups represent private interests, state and local governments also form interest groups. Most states and large cities have at least one Washington lobbyist and organizations such as the U.S. Conference of Mayors, the National Governors Conference, and the National Association of Counties work to promote the interests of state and local governments in the formulation of national policies.

2. How do interest groups promote their political goals?

When people who share similar political objectives join together and organize an interest group they have much more political clout than if each person tried to act alone. Interest groups are very involved in the political process and use different activities to promote their political goals.

- **Influencing elections** Interest groups endorse candidates, urge their members to vote for the endorsed candidates and, most importantly, form PACs and contribute money to candidates they support.

- **Lobbying** Lobbying encompasses the contacts interest groups have with elected representatives and federal officials to influence their positions and actions. See Question 3 below.

- **Litigation** Interest groups initiate lawsuits when they believe it is an effective way to advance their goals. For example, GLBT groups may challenge GLBT discrimination in court, or environment groups may challenge polluters or federal agencies that are not, in their view, adequately carrying out anti-pollution laws.

- **Coalition building** Often, interest groups try to gain support from other interest groups with similar political goals. Many different interest groups have similar political goals and may work together. The Environmental Defense Fund, the Sierra Club, and the Audubon Society might work together for environmental goals, while African-American groups, Hispanic groups, and GLBT groups might work together in support of hate crimes legislation.

- **Influencing public opinion** An interest group may publicize its issues when it believes public opinion will help advance its goals. Other times, an interest group will avoids general publicity when it feels the public will not support its goals. For example, agricultural interest groups may strive to involve their members on the issue of federal agricultural subsidies, but avoid publicizing this issue more broadly due to the lack of public support for it.

3. How do interest groups lobby?

Interest groups hire lobbyists whose job is to communicate with members of Congress and federal officials to influence legislation or federal regulations. Although the term "lobby" has a negative connotation, lobbying does not usually involve bribery or corruption. Contrary to the widespread assumptions, it involves working with supportive officials much more than applying pressure to unsupportive officials to change their minds. Here are the most important activities lobbyists engage in:

- **Providing information** The main lobbying activity of interest groups is providing information to Congress and federal agencies through reports and studies, congressional hearings, and personal communications. Of course, interest groups generally only provide information that supports their positions.

- **Building personal relationships with legislators and federal officials** The most effective lobbyists are those with strong personal relationships with key federal officials and members of Congress. Access to legislators and officials who can impact the group's agenda is important because it assures that the position of the interest group will be heard.

- **Grass-roots lobbying** Lobbyists often try to organize the interest group's membership and encourage them to contact their senators and representatives. This is done to convince legislators that the people of their district support the interest group's position and will be watching how their representative votes. If a sufficient number of individuals get involved, grass-roots lobbying can be very effective in helping the interest group influence legislation.

4. How are interest groups regulated?

In the United States, the right to form groups and get involved in the political process is a basic right and part of the political culture. However, since 1946 there have been some restrictions on interest groups and lobbying. Under the Lobbying Disclosure Act (1995), lobbyists must register with the government, and groups that lobby must disclose how they spend their money and where it is coming from. Interest groups are prohibited from donating money directly to a candidate's election campaign but may form a political action committee (PAC) to do so. However, there are limits on how much they may contribute to any one candidate and the sources and destinations of all funds must be disclosed. As a result of *Citizens United v. Federal Elections Commission* (2010), there are no limits on the amounts corporations, including interest groups, business corporations, labor unions, etc., can spend on their own efforts (independent of the candidate's campaign) to influence an election.

5. What are the advantages and disadvantages of the interest group system?

American politics, pluralist theory holds, is the struggle among a multitude of different special interests to determine public policy. Many pluralists argue that this is good—that out of the struggle between competing interest groups comes compromise and national public policies that promote the collective good. However, others argue that the system is flawed in that it gives preference to the best-funded and best-organized groups.

For example, a law requiring window stickers on used cars to list known defects had the support of an overwhelming majority of Americans but was repealed after a campaign by the National Association of Automobile Dealers that included more than $1 million in campaign contributions. The large majority that supported the law was unorganized, underfunded, and largely unaware of what was happening. One effect of the interest group system has been a weakening of majority rule; policies are often determined by the special interest group that, due to its organization and funding, has the most clout in a policy area. Critics of the interest group system point out that almost two-thirds of Washington lobbying groups are business-related and that large corporations, due to their ability to fund political contributions and lobbying activities, disproportionately influence public policy in their areas of interest.

Landmark Supreme Court Cases

Citizens United v. Federal Elections Commission (2010) Overturned limits for the amount both for-profit corporations (which includes most businesses) and not-for-profit corporations (which includes most interest group organizations) could spend on their own efforts to elect a candidate they have endorsed. See "Landmark Supreme Court Decisions" on page 163.

Topic 9 Review

1. Which branches of government do interest groups try to influence?

    A.   the legislative branch only
    B.   the executive branch only
    C.   the legislative and executive branches only
    D.   the legislative, executive, and judicial branches
    E.   the legislative and judicial branches only

2. In addition to lobbying, interest groups generally do all of the following EXCEPT

    A.   trying to get their supports elected to public office
    B.   filing lawsuits in an attempt to get the courts to further their agenda
    C.   conducting public relations efforts—sometimes including television advertising—to influence public opinion
    D.   trying to get the support of other interest groups
    E.   starting their own political parties

3. Grassroots lobbying is best described as

    A.   encouraging the interest group's membership to vote for a candidate the interest group supports

    B.   trying to get the general public to support the interest group's position on proposed legislation

    C.   conducting public opinion polling and using the results to convince senators and representatives that voters support the interest group's position

    D.   encouraging the interest group's membership to contact their senators and representatives in support of the its position on proposed legislation

    E.   organizing demonstrations or protest marches in support of the interest group's position at locations across the country, that is strong enough to have the support of the president, Congress, and the Supreme Court in advancing its policy goals

4. Which of the following statements best describes an iron triangle?

    A.   a support group consisting of the interest group's membership, related interest groups, and the interest group's leadership working together to more effectively lobby Congress

    B.   the strategy of lobbying all three branches of government at once, thereby making the interest group more effective

    C.   a network of people representing Congress, federal agencies, and the interest group itself, who work together to promote the policy goals of the interest group

    D.   a network formed by key members of a House and Senate standing committees, and the interest group leadership that effectively writes legislation supportive of the interest group's policy goals.

    E.   an interest group, such as the National Rifle Association (NRA)

Topic 10: Political Culture and the Mass Media

Before tackling this in-depth review, make sure you've reviewed the key terms relating to political culture and the mass media.

1. What values or beliefs are part of American political culture?

Political culture refers to the basic political values and beliefs shared by virtually all the population. A country's political system is based in its political culture. In general terms, it is impossible to translate the political system of one country to a different country with a radically different political culture. Here are some of the values and beliefs that make up American political culture and form the basis for the American political system:

- An acceptance of the rule of law
- The belief that all citizens are equal before the law
- The idea of limited government
- The acceptance of majority rule
- The belief in individual rights
- A high regard for the Constitution
- A high value placed on the right to own private property
- A belief in the importance of compromise to settle disagreements

2. How is a person's political identity determined?

Political socialization is the process by which an individual acquires her/his political beliefs and identity. Political socialization is the process that determines whether a person will be active in the political process or have feelings of political apathy or political alienation. Political socialization is also the process through which a person acquires an identity as a Democrat, Republican, or independent. The most important factor in the political socialization process is one's family; for example, when both parents identify with the same political party, it is highly likely that their children will as well. Other agents in the political socialization process are schools, group affiliations, the mass media, and the influence of opinion leaders.

3. What role does ideology play in the political process?

A person's core set of values and beliefs—his/her ideology—forms the basis for the person's interpretation of events and views on political, social, and economic issues. A person's ideology is acquired through the political socialization process. Differences in ideologies are often described in terms of liberal versus conservative (or "left" versus "right"). In the United States the term "conservative" as used today generally describes people who prefer a more limited role for government in the economy and society (opposing government regulation and tax increases), favor an aggressive defense policy, and support "traditional" values (prayer in schools, a ban on abortion, marriage for male-female couples only, etc.) The term "liberal" in the United States today generally applies to people who believe that government needs to play an active role in the economy and society, prefer international diplomacy over military action, and are open to social change such as same-sex civil unions or marriage. It is possible to be a conservative on social issues but at the same time take a liberal position on political and economic issues or vice versa.

4. What is the political spectrum?

The political spectrum consists of the range of political ideologies within a political system. In classic terms, the political spectrum contains these groups:

- **Radicals** (or the far left of the political spectrum) People who favor rapid, fundamental change in the existing social, economic, and/or political order.
- **Liberals** (or the area left of center in the political spectrum) People who support an active government that works to address national problems and produce some social and political change.
- **Moderates** (or the middle of the political spectrum) People who fall between liberal and conservative. A democratic government is most stable when many people identify with the middle of the spectrum rather than when the system is polarized between left and right with few people in the middle.
- **Conservatives** (or the area right of center in the political spectrum) People who believe in a limited role of government in attacking national problems and support the upholding of traditional values rather than social or political change.
- **Reactionaries** (or the far right of the political spectrum) People who favor undoing social and political change and returning to a previous state of affairs.

5. What roles do the mass media play in the U.S. political system?

The mass media play a key role in the U.S. political system; in fact, they are so important that they have even been called the "fourth branch of government." Among the functions they perform in the political process are:

- **Informing the public** The mass media provide the means through which the citizens are informed of the actions of government and the issues under consideration by the government.

- **Setting the national agenda** The mass media, in determining what news to cover, play a role in deciding what issues will get national attention and thus influence the national agenda.

- **Serving as a watchdog on government activities** Different news sources compete to be the first to uncover and report scandal or malfeasance on the part of government officials, helping to keep government honest and responsive.

- **Providing a means for the government to communicate with citizens** Through the mass media, government officials can speak directly to large numbers of people. For example, presidents can make speeches to the public, candidates can debate before voters, and senators can be interviewed on television or in print.

- **Communicating public opinion to government officials** Different news outlets (such as newspapers, television networks, and websites) can reflect the opinions of the public on national issues by interviewing citizens for news stories, publishing letters to the editor, and commissioning public opinion polls.

6. How do the press and the government interact?

The news media today focuses on the president. Congress gets much less coverage and the Supreme Court gets coverage only when an important case is being decided. In contrast, the daily actions of the president—and even the president's spouse—are usually covered in detail. Presidents interact with the news media in a number of ways, including announcements issued as press releases, speeches (the text of which is usually given to reporters in advance), and, occasionally, an interview with a reporter. In addition, the White House press secretary generally holds daily news briefings with reporters in which announcements are made and reporters ask questions. Presidents or congressional leaders sometimes hold press conferences to answer the questions of reporters. Political leaders or their staff may also grant personal interviews. In an interview or news briefing held by any government official, information provided "off the record" may not be made public and information provided "not for attribution" may be printed but the source cannot be identified. A "leak" is the unauthorized release of information by a government official that was intended to remain secret. Sometimes a "leak" may actually be intentionally authorized by government officials as a means of testing an idea with the public. For example, a White House official might tell a reporter "off the record" that a controversial idea is being considered; if the public reaction is strongly negative, the White House can shift course and deny it was ever considering the idea.

7. How does the government regulate broadcast journalism?

The government does not regulate the dissemination of news through newspapers, magazines, and the Internet. However, the Federal Communications Commission (FCC), an independent regulatory agency, regulates broadcast news (TV and radio)—regulation that is based on the idea that radio frequencies are publicly owned. Before the rise of cable TV, when the number of television stations available was very limited for most people, the FCC required television and radio news broadcasts to abide by the Fairness Doctrine, which required that the news be reported objectively and that both sides of an issue get aired.

With the rise of multiple television and radio news networks, the Fairness Doctrine was discontinued in 1987 and objectivity in news coverage on television and radio is no longer required. The Equal Time rule, however, is still enforced. It requires television and radio stations to treat candidates for public office equally. If one candidate is given free air time to make a statement, his/her opponents must be given the same. The Equal Time rule is generally waived by the FCC for debates between Democratic and Republican presidential candidates so that television networks need not give equal time to all minor third party presidential candidates.

8. How has the delivery of news changed as a result of the rise of cable TV and the Internet as sources of news?

The rise of multiple cable television networks and multiple sources of news on the Internet has revolutionized the delivery of news in the United States during the last 25 years. Print journalism is in decline as more people rely on television and the Internet for their news. The era of objective journalism has waned and partisanship plays a growing role in the delivery of news. Since the delivery of news is controlled by for-profit companies whose profits depend on the size of their audience, many cable TV and Internet news sources have made news delivery more partisan and entertainment-oriented in an effort to increase profits in a crowded and competitive market. The result is a growth in the airing of political views on TV, radio, and the Internet, but a decline in the objectivity of news delivery. Americans' perceptions of political affairs depend on the news sources they follow. The result is a lack of a common version of reality—a situation that has contributed to greater polarization in the nation's politics.

Topic 10 Review

1. Which one of the following is a core value of American political culture?

    A.   the acceptance of majority rule

    B.   a conservative position on political issues

    C.   support of stem-cell research

    D.   identification with a political party

    E.   agreement on the proper size and role of the federal government

2. Which one of the following is NOT determined by the political socialization process?

    A.   a person's political party identification

    B.   a person's liberal/conservative ideology

    C.   whether or not a person votes or becomes involved in the political process

    D.   whether or not a person gets married at a young age

    E.   a person's view of his/her role in the political process

3. One result widely attributed, at least in part, to the rise of partisan journalism is

    A.   increased political polarization

    B.   the growing focus on fundraising in political campaigns

    C.   a decline in political participation

    D.   a growing role for the Internet in the political process

    E.   growing support for same-sex marriage

4. Which of the following is NOT a role the mass media plays in the American political system?

  A. informing the public of government activities

  B. making public policy

  C. determining what issues are important and will be reported on

  D. exposing cases of corruption and the abuse of power

  E. making it easier for candidates to communicate with the voters

Topical Review Answers and Explanations

Topic 1

1. **D.** Choices E and B are results of *McCulloch v. Maryland* rather than *Marbury v. Madison*. Judicial review is not a power mentioned in the Constitution (answer choice A) and the Supreme Court must wait until a law is passed and a case challenging it has worked its way through the federal court system before considering its constitutionality (answer choice C).

2. **C.** Only the president can nominate federal judges. All the other statements correctly describe ways Congress can check the power of the president.

3. **B.** Be careful not to confuse the separation of powers with checks and balances (answer choice A). Checks and balances requires the separation of powers but goes further by creating mechanisms for each branch to check the power of the others.

4. **E.** C sounds plausible but the principle of constitutionalism does not actually require a written constitution (it can be a series of laws or judicial precedents) and many constitutions, including that of the United States, have never actually been approved by the people.

Topic 2

1. **B.** Dual federalism is the concept that both state and federal governments have their own policy areas that they control. See chapter three for explanations of all the terms in the answer choices.

2. **A.** Concurrent powers are ones that both the federal and state governments can exercise. Taxation is not an implied power (answer choice B) since the Constitution explicitly grants Congress this power. Reserved powers (answer choice C) are powers reserved for state governments. Fiscal federalism (answer choice D) isn't directly related to the power to levy taxes; it involves giving federal grants to state and local government to carry out shared public policy objectives. While taxation can be a tool of fiscal policy, taxation is not related to monetary policy (answer choice E).

3. **A.** Judicial review was not an issue in *McCulloch v. Maryland*; it had been established sixteen years earlier by the Court's decision in *Marbury v. Madison* (1803). All of the other answer choices correctly describe *McCulloch v. Maryland*.

4. **E.** Devolution is correctly described only in this answer choice.

Topic 3

1. **E.** The Supreme Court, not Congress, adjudicates disputes between states. All other answer choices correctly describe functions of Congress.

2. **C.** Senators were chosen by state legislatures. Since 1913, senators have been chosen by a popular vote in each state, which by 1913 included all adult males over 21 years of age, and in some states, females as well.

3. **B.** Seats in the House of Representatives are reapportioned to the states based on their population as determined in a new national census and then state governments draw the congressional districts for the number of representatives they are allocated. Thus redistricting can only be done *after* seats are reapportioned to the

states (answer choice A). The Supreme Court and Congress (answer choices C and D) are not involved in the redistricting process. Answer choice E sounds plausible but it is incorrect because seats in the Senate are never subject to either reapportionment or redistricting. Each state always gets two seats in the Senate and senators are elected by a statewide vote for which no districts need to be drawn.

4. **D.** Congressmen, in order to get reelected generally must first take into account the interests of their district rather than the broad national interest. All other answer choices correctly describe Congress.

Topic 4

1. **D.** All the answer choices describe reasons that the president finds it difficult to control the bureaucracy except answer choice D. The president *can* fire key officials of the executive branch that the Senate has approved. Of federal officials nominated by the president and approved by the Senate, the president is restricted from firing only federal judges and the officials of independent regulatory agencies.

2. **B.** The FTC writes and enforces federal regulations to protect consumers and prevent anti-competitive business practices. But unlike most agencies of the executive branch it is not under the control of the president. Commissioners are nominated by the president and approved by Congress but they serve staggered seven-year terms, cannot be removed only by impeachment, and only three of the five commissioners can be from the same political party. Other independent regulatory agencies, such as the Securities and Exchange Commission, Federal Reserve Board, and Federal Communications Commission, are structured similarly. Answer choices A, D, and E are all part of the departmental structure of the federal government under the control of the president and are not considered independent. The USPS (answer choice D) is independent but it is a governmental corporation rather than a regulatory agency.

3. **A.** Mandatory spending refers to spending on entitlement programs, which is spending required (mandated) by law. Spending on interest on the national debt (answer choice C) does not fit the definition of mandatory spending but is considered compulsory spending. Spending on national defense and homeland security (answer choices D and E) is termed discretionary spending since it is not mandated by law; Congress must approve it each year. Although the president is required to spend earmarked funds (answer choice B), this also is part of the category of discretionary spending because earmarks are inserted into the budget at the discretion of Congress; they are not required by federal law.

4. **B.** As commander in chief of the U.S. military, the president can send troops abroad without Congressional approval. This is true even under the War Powers Resolution, which attempted to limit the president's power to wage war without approval by Congress.

Topic 5

1. **B.** If four of the nine Supreme Court vote to hear a case being appealed to the Supreme Court, the Court takes the case. If not, the decision of the lower court stands.

2. **C.** Both the U.S. Courts of Appeal and the Supreme Court are appellate courts that hear cases appealed to them from lower courts. The U.S. District Courts are courts of original jurisdiction (answer choices A and D).

3. **E.** Stare decisis is the term applied to the principle that courts should follow precedents set in previous decisions. The term that applies to answer choice B is judicial restraint; there are no commonly used terms to describe the principles stated in the other incorrect answer choices.

4. **C.** Civil law refers to laws governing relations between private parties where no criminal act is involved. Criminal law defines crimes and, under these laws, the government arrests persons accused of

a crime and prosecutes these people in court (answer choice D). Both state governments (answer choice B) and the federal government create both civil and criminal law.

Topic 6

1. **D.** The Fifth and Sixth Amendments describe rights of persons accused of a crime. *Miranda v. Arizona* (answer choice E) did not establish these rights but only required that persons accused of a crime be informed of their rights.

2. **C.** The right to privacy was first recognized by the Supreme Court in *Griswold v. Connecticut* (1965), which declared a state law prohibiting the use of birth control devices to be unconstitutional. Answer choices A and B are subsequent Court decisions based on the right to privacy recognized in *Griswold v. Connecticut*. Answer choices D and E are cases unrelated to the right of privacy.

3. **D.** The Court's decision in *District of Columbia v. Heller* reversed previous decisions that had held that the constitutional right to bear arms applied only to service in a state militia and declared instead that the Second Amendment granted a broad general right to gun ownership. The case did not address gun registration, gun purchasing, or restrictions on carrying guns.

4. **E.** The "excessive entanglement with religion test" is applied by the courts to determine if a government action violates the establishment clause of the First Amendment. In actual practice, the separation of church and state is blurred and not a complete separation (answer choice A). Applying the excessive-entanglement test, the Supreme Court has held that government can provide school vouchers that allow students to attend parochial schools at government expense, can fund buildings at private church-supported colleges that are not used for religious purposes, and can fund programs run by religious organizations as long as such activities do not excessively entangle government with religion or give preference to certain religions over others.

Topic 7

1. **B.** Suffrage refers to the right to vote and the women's suffrage movement sought the right to vote.

2. **C.** The decision held that strict racial quotas could not be used to create racial balance, although the goal of creating racial balance could still be a factor in its admissions policy. The decision in *University of California Regents v. Bakke* did not eliminate all affirmative action programs (answer choice D), but subsequent decisions of the Court have gone much further in that direction. In *Grutter v. Bollinger* (2003), the Supreme Court held that race could be used as one factor in college admissions (along with ethnic identity, gender, etc.) to ensure the diversity conducive to a quality education (but not to create racial balance).

3. **C.** Poll taxes were eliminated by the Twenty-Fourth Amendment and literacy tests by the Voting Rights Act of 1965. The poll tax and literacy tests were eliminated by the federal government, not the states (answer choice A); in fact many states with poll taxes and literacy tests for voting, fought the federal government on this issue, championing the idea of states rights. Loving v. Virginia eliminated state laws prohibiting interracial marriage (answer choice B) and the Civil Rights Act of 1964 (answer choice D) eliminated racial segregation in public accommodations but had nothing to do with the poll tax and literacy tests. An executive order cannot be used to eliminate poll taxes or literacy tests since they are orders issued by the president to the departments/agencies that are under his authority (answer choice E); an example is President Truman's executive order issued to the military desegregating the armed forces.

4. **A.** Reed v. Reed was a case in civil law between a divorced couple; the Court's decision eliminated preferences granted males over females in many state laws.

Topic 8

1. **C.** Answer choice A describes a closed primary and answer choice B describes a blanket primary (used only in Washington and California). No state allows voters to vote on more than one ballot (answer choice D).

2. **E.** In spite of the decline in power of the Democratic and Republican Parties, there has been no surge in third parties—either in their membership or the number of third parties. All of the other answer choices correctly describe reasons the power of political parties is in decline.

3. **D.** Presidential candidates focus on swing states since a "swing" of just a few voters could mean a pick up of all the state's electoral votes. It does a candidate no good to increase their support in states they would carry anyway (answer choice A) or to increase their support in states they are going to lose anyway (answer choice B). Unless a large state is a swing state, the presidential candidates will not do much campaigning there except to raise money to be spent in swing states; in recent elections the three largest states (listed in answer choice C) have been largely ignored by the candidates except for fundraising.

4. **C.** African-Americans, labor union members, and people under 30 are all more likely to vote Democratic than the general population. Whites, business owners, and males all are more likely to vote Republican.

Topic 9

1. **D.** Most interest groups focus on the legislative and executive branches but do not hesitate to use litigation (judicial branch) if it will advance their policy goals. In fact, some interest groups, such as the ACLU (civil liberties), Environmental Defense Fund (environmental protection), and Lambda Legal (GLBT rights), focus entire effort to advance their policy goals on the judicial branch.

2. **E.** Only in unusual circumstances has an interest group formed a political party; the Free-Soil, Greenback, and Prohibition Parties are historical examples of single-issue parties representing a particular interest group. All of the other answer choices are activities that interest groups commonly get involved in.

3. **D.** Grass-roots lobbying involves getting an interest group's members to do the lobbying—a tactic that can be very successful since most senators and representatives pay attention to the views of their constituents.

4. **C.** An iron triangle is a network of key people in Congress, federal agencies, and the interest group itself that work together to advance the public policy goals of the interest group. An interest group that successfully forms an iron triangle can wield considerable influence on public policy.

Topic 10

1. **A.** Majority rule is a core value that virtually all Americans accept as basis of our government. Answer choices B, and E are basic values or beliefs but not ones shared by nearly all Americans; thus, they are not part of our political culture. Answer choice C involves an issue on which people disagree rather than a basic value or core belief that forms part of a political culture. A third of Americans do not identify with any political party, so answer choice D is also not a core value of our political culture.

2. **D.** The age at which a person gets married is not directly related to the political process and thus not determined by political socialization. All of the other answer choices are results of the political socialization process which creates each person's unique political beliefs, values, world outlook, and identity.

3. **A.** Americans no longer depend on a few common news sources for their information regarding politics and government. As news sources have multiplied, many people have chosen to get their

news from a source that shares their views and biases. Most observers believe this has been one factor contributing to increased political polarization. None of the other answer choices have any apparent relationship to partisan journalism.

4. **B.** The mass media perform all the functions listed except making public policy. Of course the information the mass media provides can influence others in making public policy, but the mass media itself is not directly involved.

THE BIG PICTURE: HOW TO PREPARE YEAR-ROUND

The AP U.S. Government and Politics Exam may be months away, but the time to start preparing is now. This section will help you to register for the test, prepare for the test in class and out, personalize your test prep plan, and manage the stress an AP test brings. As the test gets closer, you can use the materials throughout this book to help you review what you've already learned. When the night before the exam arrives, you'll be ready to earn a top score.

Deciding to Take the AP Test

You are probably well aware of the advantages of taking Advanced Placement (AP) courses in high school. AP courses and exams provide college-bound high school students the opportunity to take a college-level course. Taking an AP course demonstrates you're serious about learning and about college. For that reason, many colleges, in deciding whether or not to admit you to their freshman class, will consider, among other things, the AP courses you took. Taking an AP course will also help you experience the difficulty level of a college course and see if you're ready.

However, the real benefits of the AP program come from doing well on an AP test. If you score high enough on the test, nearly all colleges and universities will grant college credit for your AP course. This means you enter college having already earned some college credit—a fact that can save you both time and money. If you get AP credits, you're already on the road to a college degree and you can take fewer courses—and pay less money—when you're actually in college.

Each college determines its own policy regarding AP exams. Some colleges and universities grant credits to students getting a score of 3 on the test, but most grant college credit only to students who get a score of 4 or 5. Check with the colleges you are considering to see what their specific policies are toward the AP U.S. Government and Politics Exam. Colleges usually post this information on their websites.

Registering for the Test

The AP U.S. Government and Politics test is offered once a year on a date early in May. If unusual circumstances make it impossible for you to test on that date, you may be able to take the test during the late-testing period later in the month.

If you are enrolled in an AP U.S. Government and Politics course in your school, the test will probably be offered in your school. In that case, your AP teacher or an AP coordinator at your school will make the arrangements and supervise the test registration process.

However, you can take the AP U.S. Government and Politics Exam even if you are not enrolled in the course. Each year hundreds of students who are home-schooled or who study independently take the AP U.S. Government and Politics Exam. In fact, some states sponsor online AP courses specifically for students at schools that don't offer the AP U.S. Government and Politics course. If you wish to take the AP exam but are not enrolled in a course at a school, you will need to contact the College Board to locate a nearby school offering the test and then contact the test coordinator at that school to make arrangements.

Here are some important tips for the registration process:

1. **Get the right information.** Refer to the College Board's official websites for the information you need about the test, including eligibility for late testing, special accommodations for students with disabilities, reduced testing fees for students who can't afford the fee ($87 in 2011), etc. Don't rely on what your friends say or even necessarily what your teacher says, since requirements and procedures may have changed. This site also has information about sending your score on the AP exam to colleges and universities. Go to www.collegeboard.com.

2. **Start the registration process early.** You don't want to miss the one opportunity each year to take the test. If you are enrolled in an AP course, ask your teacher in January or February about registering for the test if this hasn't already been explained and discussed in class. If you are *not* enrolled in a formal AP class in a school, you will need to take the initiative and contact the College Board before March 1 to find out what school nearby is administering the AP U.S. Government and Politics Exam and then contact the school's AP coordinator to register.

3. **Register for the correct test.** Make sure to register for U.S. Government and Politics, not U.S. History (or something else). You don't want to find out too late that you've wasted months of valuable study time.

Thinking About Not Taking the Test?

You have little to lose if you don't do well on the test, and a lot to gain if you do get a good score. You may do better than you expected, especially if you are able to study and review before the test date. If you don't do well, you can cancel your score free of charge (but the test fee is not refunded) and the score will not appear on AP score reports the College Board sends to colleges (check www.collegeboard.com for details).

A low test score means you won't get college credit, but it will generally not hurt your admission chances. Colleges still value the fact you chose to challenge yourself by taking an AP course. Of course, you won't get the testing fee back if you don't score high enough to earn college credit. But if you do well, you will have made one of the best investments of your life, considering the cost of college credits at both public and private institutions of higher learning.

Using Your AP Class to Score Well on the Test

Most students who do well in the AP class also do well on the AP exam. But doing well in class won't necessarily mean you'll do well on the test. The skills and techniques required in a class are not exactly the same as those required for a standardized timed multiple-choice or timed essay test. If you want get the most out of the class in terms of what you need to succeed on the standardized AP test, here are some tips and strategies you can use:

1. **Take AP U.S. History.** It's helpful to take AP U.S. History before AP U.S. Government and Politics. A good grounding in U.S. history will be of enormous value in AP U.S. Government and Politics, in which you'll be expected to understand the history that gave rise to the creation of the U.S. Constitution and understand constitutional amendments and landmark Supreme Court decisions in their historical context. A good background in U.S. history is also important to understanding the evolution of federalism, the development of democracy, the struggle for equal rights by African Americans, and the changing role of government in American life. Ideally you should take AP U.S. Government and Politics right after you take AP U.S. History. Or, if you can handle the workload, consider taking the two classes at the same time, since there is some overlap between the two courses.

2. **Focus on the facts.** The AP U.S. Government and Politics Exam primarily tests facts. Throughout your AP class, try to get the facts

straight and remember them. You'll need to know how Congress, the Supreme Court, and the executive branch are set up, how a bill becomes a law, how political parties and interest groups behave, how the Supreme Court has interpreted the Constitution, etc. But you won't need to take a stand on a controversial issue and defend it. You won't be tested on your research skills or debating skills. You won't have to read a political essay or a presidential speech and analyze it or interpret it. You may be assigned interpretive readings in class but for the AP test you won't have to remember these authors or their positions. These things may be part of your AP course grade, but they won't be things you need to do for the AP U.S. Government and Politics Exam.

3. **Focus on the federal government and the national political process, not state governments.** Federalism and the relationship between national and state governments is always a key concept tested on the AP exam. This topic often appears in several multiple choice questions as well as in the free-response section of the test. Make sure you understand federalism and different interpretations of this concept. But on the AP test you won't be asked any questions about your state government (or other state governments). Any readings or discussions regarding your state government in class may be part of your grade in the class, but this won't be on the AP test.

4. **Know the Constitution.** It's helpful to actually read the Constitution; it's not too long or too difficult. Get your own copy (you can find it online and print it out) and mark it up with notes as you go through your course. Make sure you understand all the terms in the Constitution. It's also helpful to know what each of the amendments changed and why each of them was adopted. You are certain to impress essay graders if you can refer in specific terms to the articles and amendments of the Constitution in your essays. Practice doing this in discussions and written exercises in your class.

5. **Be sure you understand landmark Supreme Court decisions.** Landmark Supreme Court decisions interpret the Constitution. Be especially alert and attentive any time a Supreme Court case is discussed in class, and ask questions when you don't understand. It's not enough just to memorize the decision in the case. For each landmark case, learn the facts of the case, the decision reached, the grounds on which the decision is based (the language in the Constitution), and the long-term significance of the decision. Practice referring to relevant Supreme Court cases by name when making your points in class discussions, essays, and tests. Landmark Supreme Court decisions will be the focus of several multiple-choice questions of the official AP U.S. Government and Politics Exam. You should also be able to incorporate Supreme Court decisions into your responses to the essay questions in Section II of the test.

6. **Make sure you've covered all the necessary subject areas.** The AP test is administered early in May and you may not be done with your AP class until well into June. If you haven't covered all chapters of your textbook (except state government) by the time of the test, you may need to work ahead. You can use this book to get the basics of any subject area you haven't covered in class or that you missed. Also, be aware that during the week before the test, AP teachers often rush to make sure all the necessary content has been covered in your course. This can be a problem if you have procrastinated and are trying to cram as much review of earlier chapters into the last week before the test as well. Try to complete your test prep content review one week before the test, so you can use the last week to focus on any new content being covered in your class.

Personalizing Your Test Prep Plan

The fact that you're taking an AP class means that you are probably a busy high school student trying to fit in time for classes, homework, extracurricular activities, your social life, and family obligations. You probably have only limited time for review for the AP U.S. Government and Politics Exam. This section will help you get the most out of your limited test preparation time and make it really count.

You need a plan specifically for you—one that addresses your needs in the time you have available. The strategies below are designed to help you adapt the Fast-Track or Complete Test Prep Plan to meet your needs. No two people will have exactly the same plan or use this book in exactly the same way. To develop a personalized test prep plan, you'll need to identify your weak points and then allocate time to address them efficiently and effectively. Here are the three basic steps to creating your own personalized test prep plan:

1. **Identify your weak points.** Start by taking an AP U.S. Government and Politics practice test. This will let you know what you're up against. It will also help you get a feel for the exam and identify the subject areas that you most need to focus on. Based on your performance on the practice test you can prioritize what subjects you need to review, starting with the areas in which you are weakest.

   If you time is limited or you feel you're not ready to take a complete practice test, another way to get a sense of where you need to focus your review is to skim the chapter on key terms and identify those subject areas in which you have the most difficulty understanding the terms.

2. **Develop a review plan and a schedule.** Figure out how much time you can devote each week to test preparation and reserve specific blocks of time for this purpose. After you've identified the areas you most need to focus on, create a written schedule that includes specific time slots and specific activities or content areas you want to review in each time slot. This will help you pace yourself to get through all the material you want to review. There are probably content areas or question types you want to focus on more than others. But make sure your plan includes time to not only review content, but also to master the strategies and take practice tests.

Use the Last-Minute Study Guide or the Comprehensive Review as a starting point, adding time in those content areas you are weak and skipping over areas you are confident you know. There is no right and wrong plan for everyone. In fact, your test prep plan should be unique because it should reflect the time you have, the content areas you want to review, and the way you like to study.

3. **Marshal your self-discipline!** The hard part about a test prep plan is making sure you stick to it. Schedule your test prep time and then schedule other things around it so it doesn't get pushed aside by other activities. You've come a long way; now don't blow the test by not being prepared. Develop a plan for your needs and the time you have available and then stay with it.

For some people, it helps to have a study partner. This may make it easier to hold to the schedule and it may also help you study better. You and your study partner can quiz each other, share information, and exchange ideas. However, for other people, having a study partner makes it harder to stay on topic and focus on studying. Try to figure out, based on past experience, how you can best enforce your study plan and most effectively use your time.

Managing Test Stress

It's only natural to feel some stress over the AP test—you've invested a lot into it. Some people test best under stress. They use the adrenalin to increase their pace and pump up their brain energy level. Others, however, are overwhelmed by it. Stress may cause their minds to race uncontrollably, keep them from concentrating and thinking clearly, and cause them to freeze up and forget things they know. In extreme cases, text anxiety can even make people physically ill. Studies have shown that a high level of test anxiety can overwhelm students and prevent them from getting the score they would otherwise be capable of. If stress sometimes overwhelms you and you feel it keeps you from doing your best on an important test, the following suggestions may help.

1. **Be prepared.** Of course, you'll be more confident and less stressed out if you are prepared for the test. Use your stress level to motivate you to start preparing well in advance and ease up the last week before the test. Avoid cramming and use the last week for activities that well help you relax and build confidence. Try to reassure yourself with how well prepared you are. Keep in mind, however, that preparation alone may not work; for people with serious test anxiety, the more they prepare, the more stressed they may become.

2. **Imagine yourself succeeding.** Text anxiety can become a vicious cycle: the more you worry about it, the more stressed out you become. The only way to conquer test anxiety is to think positively instead of letting anxiety control you. Banish negative thoughts from your brain and imagine yourself succeeding. Think about how good you can do rather than thinking about failing.

3. **Breathe deeply.** Breathing exercises can be useful in helping you to relax when anxiety overwhelms you. Practice breathing exercises and relaxation techniques. If you have an anxiety attack while taking the test, breath deeply and focus on positive thoughts (see #2 above). Taking long deep breaths will help you control your physical reaction to stress and help you regain control.

4. **Accept mistakes and move on.** Almost no one gets all the questions right; in fact, it's possible to miss quite a few questions and still get a score of 5 on an AP test. During the test don't worry about the questions you don't know or think you missed. Move on and focus on the questions you can get right. If you've blanked out on a question for which you know the answer, skip the question and come back to it later.

5. **Seek help.** If you feel text anxiety is a serious problem for you and you can't control it on your own, talk to a counselor, teacher, or parent about getting help. Counseling may help and there are techniques you can learn such as centering. Actors, musicians, Olympic athletes, and others who need to achieve peak performance under

extreme pressure are often trained in this technique. Remember that anxiety and stress are common problems, so don't be shy about asking for help.

Resources for Further Study

Books

The **United States Constitution**—Word for word, the Constitution is the single best resource for studying U.S. Government and Politics. Study it and mark it up as you work your way through your class.

Barron's AP Government and Politics—This book provides strong, comprehensive coverage of the most common topics tested in the exam. The book includes two practice tests, and two more practice tests can be found in an optional CD-ROM.

Online

www.mymaxscore.com/aptests—At this site, you can take another free AP practice test. Detailed answers and explanations are provided for both the multiple-choice and free-response sections.

www.collegeboard.com/student/testing/ap/sub_usgov.html—At the College Board site, you can find sample tests, advice, and general information about the exam. You'll find it particularly useful to review the last several years' worth of essay prompts, which are provided for free on the site. Full tests are available for sale.

This book contains one practice test. Visit mymaxscore.com to download your free second practice test with answers and explanations.

AP U.S. Government and Politics Practice Exam

Section I

Time—45 minutes

60 questions

Directions: Each of the following questions or incomplete statements below is followed by five suggested answers or completions. Select the best answer in each case.

1. Which statement correctly describes a check on the power of the president?

    A. Congress can override a presidential veto of legislation by a majority vote in both houses.

    B. The Supreme Court can review executive orders as they are issued to determine their constitutionality.

    C. The House of Representatives can reject a treaty negotiated by the president.

    D. The Senate can select a federal judge the president does not support.

    E. Congress can change the president's proposed federal budget.

DEMOCRATIC AND REPUBLICAN PRESIDENTIAL VOTING PATTERNS POLL

(Expressed as a percentage of two-party vote; third-party votes are excluded)

Characteristic	1992		1996		2000		2004		2008	
	Democratic	Republican	Democratic	Republican	Democratic	Republican	Democratic	Republican	Democratic	Republican
	(percent)		(percent)		(percent)		(percent)		(percent)	
Sex:										
Male	55	45	51	49	47	53	46	54	52	48
Female	61	39	65	35	56	44	53	47	57	43
Race:										
White	52	48	51	49	46	54	42	58	44	56
Black	94	6	99	1	92	8	90	10	99	1
Education:										
Less than high school	68	32	82	18	65	35	69	31	72	28
High school diploma/ equivalent	62	38	60	40	53	47	46	54	57	43
Some college, no degree	58	42	56	44	50	50	47	53	53	47
College or advanced degree	52	48	49	51	50	50	50	50	51	49
Union household	68	32	75	25	61	39	64	36	60	40
Nonunion household	57	43	54	46	50	50	46	54	54	46

Source: Based on polling conducted by American National Election Studies

2. Which of the following statements is/are supported by the data shown in the table above?

    I.   Women tend to support the Democratic presidential candidate more than men.

    II. Blacks are more likely to vote for Democratic presidential candidates than whites.

    III. Union households tend to vote for Democratic presidential candidates.

IV. People with college degrees generally favor the Republican candidate for president.

A. Statements I, II, and III only

B. Statements I and II only

C. Statements II and III only

D. Statements II, III, and IV only

E. Statement III only

3. The term "pluralism" refers to

A. government by the people, rather than by a single dictator or king

B. the making of public policy within a multiparty system

C. the political process in which multiple interest groups compete with each other to determine public policy

D. a political system dominated by a few powerful interest groups

E. the making of public policy within a two-party system

4. When the House and Senate pass similar bills, the two versions of the legislation are merged into one bill by

A. a standing committee

B. a conference committee

C. a reconciliation committee

D. the president when he signs the bill

E. the leaders of the majority party in the House and Senate

5. The federal government's dominance over state governments in the American political system is due to all the following EXCEPT

A. the supremacy clause of the Constitution (Article VI)

B. the Tenth Amendment

C. state governments' dependence on grants from the federal government

D. the federal government's power to control interstate commerce

E. the Supreme Court's ruling in *McCulloch v. Maryland*

6. The reason the framers of the Constitution specified life terms for judges was

    A. to insulate judges from political pressures
    B. to maintain stability on the federal courts
    C. to save time by eliminating frequent confirmation hearings in the Senate
    D. to raise the average age of Supreme Court justices because they believed that with age, comes wisdom
    E. to allow justices to get to know one another over time so they could work together better

7. Which one of the following would change as a result of a constitutional amendment limiting a Senator to two terms in office?

    A. the committee system used in the Senate
    B. the selection procedure for President of the Senate
    C. the number of open seats in elections for the Senate
    D. the number of incumbents reelected to a second term in the Senate
    E. the number of African Americans in the Senate

8. Which of the following Supreme Court decisions was based on the First Amendment?

    A. *Griswold v. Connecticut* (use of birth control devices)
    B. *Gideon v. Wainwright* (lawyers for defendants who cannot afford them)
    C. *District of Columbia v. Heller* (gun ownership)
    D. *Texas v. Johnson* (flag burning)
    E. *Miranda v. Arizona* (persons accused must be informed of rights)

9. Which one of the following statements correctly describes part of the process for amending the U.S. Constitution?

    A. The president can submit a proposed amendment to the states for ratification.

    B. The people of the United States have the right to vote on changes to the Constitution.

    C. Amendments must be approved by three-fourths of the states.

    D. Congress can submit an amendment to the states for ratification if a majority of both houses support the amendment.

    E. The president can veto an amendment proposed by Congress.

10. Why do candidates generally moderate their views after winning the primary election?

    A. Candidates like to confuse their opponents by changing positions.

    B. Fundraising is usually more successful with appeals to the center of the political spectrum.

    C. Candidates, after winning the primary, usually hire political consultants, who can provide better advice.

    D. In order to win the primary, candidates need to get the support of the party's base, but to win the general election, candidates need to get support from independents.

    E. As they get more campaign experience, candidates usually realize that some of their positions are too extreme.

11. Which one of the following is NOT an option for the president when Congress passes a bill and sends it to him for his signature?

  A. The president can sign the bill into law.

  B. The president can veto the bill, in which case the bill does not become a law unless Congress overrides the veto.

  C. The president can veto part of the bill, in which case the vetoed parts of the bill do not become law unless Congress overrides the veto.

  D. The president can take no action, in which case the bill becomes a law without his signature after a 10-day period (excluding Sundays).

  E. If Congress has adjourned within 10 days of passing the bill, the president can use a "pocket veto," killing the bill without actually vetoing it.

12. The Supreme Court, in *Brown v. Board of Education of Topeka* (1954), ruled that

  A. Busing of children is required to create racial balance in public school systems.

  B. Separate schools for whites and blacks are inherently unequal.

  C. Having separate schools for blacks and whites does not violate the Constitution as long as the facilities are more or less equal.

  D. Separate facilities for whites and blacks are not appropriate but the federal government cannot get involved since education is a matter left to the states by the U.S. Constitution.

  E. Public schools cannot use a quota system to assign students to schools in order to create racial balance.

13. In terms of their power to influence the content of bills, the most important members of the House and Senate are

   A.   the chairs of the standing committees

   B.   the Speaker of the House and vice president of the United States

   C.   the majority party leaders of the House and the Senate

   D.   the members with the most knowledge and expertise on the issue under consideration

   E.   the members of each house with the most seniority

14. Which one of the following is a role that the news media do NOT perform in the American political system?

   A.   deciding which candidates will get air time for ads on radio and television and which ones won't

   B.   informing the public of what government is doing

   C.   exposing incompetent, corrupt, or hypocritical officials

   D.   focusing attention to issues and problems

   E.   providing time/space for advertisements that allow candidates to speak or send a message directly to the American public

15. All of the following are core values of American political culture EXCEPT

   A.   representative government

   B.   civilian control of the military

   C.   equality before the law of all citizens

   D.   limited government

   E.   the belief that government has gotten too big

FEDERAL GRANTS-IN-AID TO STATE AND LOCAL GOVERNMENTS

Year	Current Dollars		Constant (2000) Dollars	
	Total Grants (in $billions)	Annual percent change	Total Grants (in $billions)	Annual percent change
2000	285.9	6.6	285.9	3.7
2001	318.5	11.4	310.7	8.7
2002	352.9	10.8	338.4	8.9
2003	388.5	10.1	363.3	7.4
2004	407.5	4.9	370.4	2.0
2005	428.0	5.0	373.6	0.9
2006	434.1	1.4	364.0	-2.6
2007	443.8	2.2	361.3	-0.7
2008	461.3	3.9	357.3	-1.1
2009, estimated	567.8	23.1	440.4	23.3

Source: U.S. Office of Management and Budget

16. Which of the following statements is best supported by the data in the table above?

   A. Federal grants-in-aid to state and local governments have increased every year from 2000 to 2009, even when adjusted for inflation.

   B. Federal grants-in-aid to state and local governments, measured in current dollars, increased by about $280 million between 2000 and 2009.

   C. Before adjusting for inflation, federal grants-in-aid to state and local governments in 2009 were more than three times what they were in 2000.

   D. Before adjusting for inflation, federal grants-in-aid to state and local governments increased by 0.9% in 2005 over the previous year.

   E. The biggest annual increase in federal grants-in-aid to state and local governments occurred in 2009.

17. Which of the following statements best summarizes the trend shown in the table?

   A. Federal grants-in-aid to state and local government increased substantially between 2000 and 2009 even after adjustment for inflation.

   B. After adjusting for inflation, federal grants-in-aid to state and local governments fluctuated up and down between 2000 and 2009 with no clear long-term trend.

   C. Federal grants-in-aid are best measured in "current" dollars, since only then is the true increase from 2000 to 2009 shown.

   D. Limits should be placed on federal grants-in-aid to control federal spending and reduce the deficit.

   E. Federal grants-in-aid to state and local governments will exceed one trillion dollars by 2019.

18. What judicial philosophy best describes the decisions of the Supreme Court during the Warren Court?

   A. dual federalism
   B. doctrine of original intent
   C. judicial restraint
   D. judicial activism
   E. judicial review

19. Which of the following is a power given the vice president by the Constitution?

   A. playing a key leadership role in the Congress as President of the Senate

   B. heading the cabinet as the highest ranking U.S. official after the president

   C. breaking tie votes in the Senate

   D. representing the United States at international conferences and events when the president is unable to do so

   E. serving as a liaison between the president and Congress

20. After committee hearings are held on a bill, what is the next step in its route toward becoming a law?

   A. The committee rewrites the bill and votes on it.

   B. A subcommittee is formed to consider amendments to the bill.

   C. The Rules Committee reviews the bill and decides what rules will apply to its consideration.

   D. The Supreme Court gives an informal opinion on the bill's constitutionality.

   E. The bill goes to the other house of Congress for committee hearings there.

21. The rules governing registration and voting in federal elections are made by

   A. the Federal Election Commission

   B. federal laws enacted by Congress

   C. the Attorney General

   D. the Department of Justice

   E. each state's government

22. Which statement below best describes the national government of the United States under the Articles of Confederation?

   A. The national government was effective only because of widespread respect for the leadership of George Washington.

   B. The Supreme Court could only review cases if states requested it to.

   C. The national government consisted only of a legislative branch dominated by the larger states, which had more representatives.

   D. There were no legislative or judicial branches of government.

   E. States retained most of the power while the national government was weak and unable to act quickly in an emergency.

23. Of the thousands of cases appealed to the Supreme Court each year, the decision of which hundred or so will actually be considered by the Court is made by

   A. the Chief Justice, who sets the agenda for the Court's term

   B. the Supreme Court, which hears a case if four justices vote to hear it

   C. the Supreme Court, which hears a case only if no justice objects to hearing it

   D. the Attorney General, who decides which cases require a Supreme Court ruling

   E. the U.S. Courts of Appeals, which decide which cases are important enough to send to the Supreme Court

POLITICAL PARTY SELF-IDENTIFICATION

Party	1988	1992	1996	2000	2004
Democratic	35%	36%	37%	34%	33%
Republican	28%	25%	24%	24%	28%
Independent	36%	38%	40%	40%	39%

Source: American National Election Studies

24. Which of the following is NOT a conclusion that can be drawn from the data in the table above?

   A. More citizens of the United States identify their party affiliation as Democratic than Republican.

   B. Since 1988 the party identification of voters has seen some fluctuation, but overall there has been little change.

   C. About a third of U.S. citizens identify themselves as Democrats.

   D. Of the years shown in the table, the Democratic lead in party identification was smallest in 2004.

   E. Most people in the United States vote for Democratic candidates for president.

25. In the study of political systems, the term "political socialization" refers to the process through which

    A.   people socialize with others and engage in political activity

    B.   individuals acquire their political beliefs, values, and identity

    C.   government entitlement programs like Social Security and Medicare become popular, leading to more and more socialism

    D.   candidates try to get supporters more involved in politics as donors, campaign volunteers, etc.

    E.   social issues, such as same-sex marriage and abortion, become more important that political issues in influencing how people vote

26. What was the goal of Congress in passing the War Powers Resolution?

    A.   to eliminate the normal constitutional protections and rights of persons plotting terrorist acts

    B.   to authorize presidents to invade a foreign country if it is believed the country is manufacturing weapons of mass destruction

    C.   to give the president power to fight wars against stateless terrorist groups rather than just fighting wars against other countries

    D.   to authorize the president to order wiretapping without a court warrant if necessary in the war on terrorism

    E.   to limit the power of the president as commander in chief in committing U.S. troops to combat operations abroad

27. If no candidate for president gets a majority of electoral votes (currently 270), the president is chosen by

    A.   the House of Representatives

    B.   the Senate

    C.   a joint session of the House and the Senate

    D.   a second vote in the Electoral College between the top two candidates

    E.   the Supreme Court

28. The Supreme Court's decision in *Engle v. Vitale* regarding school prayer was based on the

    A. First Amendment right to freedom of speech
    B. Fifth Amendment right to remain silent
    C. free-exercise clause of the First Amendment
    D. establishment clause of the First Amendment
    E. right to privacy implied in the Bill of Rights

29. The Great Compromise at the Constitutional Convention was an agreement that resulted in

    A. federalism or the sharing of power between the federal government and independent state governments
    B. smaller states getting equal representation in Congress but larger states getting most of the power in the Electoral College
    C. a bicameral Congress with each state's representation equal in one house and based on population in the other house
    D. senators being chosen directly by the people but the president chosen by the Electoral College
    E. African American slaves being counted as three-fifths of a person for purposes of representation and taxation

30. Which statement best explains why third parties seldom develop much momentum in the American political system?

    A. Most political issues have only two sides—for or against—leaving no place for a third-party position.
    B. Polls show American voters are generally satisfied with the presidential candidate choices offered by the two parties.
    C. Due to single-member districts and the winner-take-all system in the Electoral College, third parties often end up with no representation in government and thus no power.
    D. Article I of the Constitution sets up the two-party system.
    E. There are almost no independent voters who might be open to a third party.

PARTICIPATION IN ELECTIONS FOR HOUSE OF REPRESENTATIVES

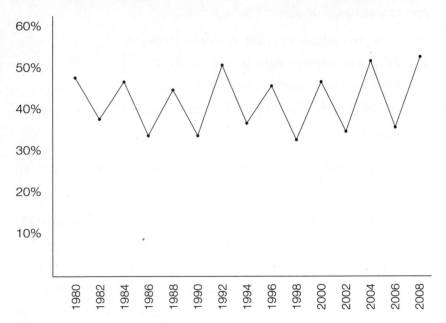

Source: American National Election Studies

31. Which is a fact that could explain the pattern shown in the line graph above?

A. Due to the staggered nature of the expiration of their terms, more seats in the House of Representatives are up for election on a four-year cycle.

B. To express their anger at the party in power, people are more likely to vote in midterm elections than in elections when the president is running.

C. The party in power usually loses seats in Congress in midterm elections.

D. More people vote in federal elections in years the president is being elected.

E. Voter turnout in elections fluctuates up and down, depending on many unpredictable factors.

32. Entitlement programs are

    A. government programs that provide benefits to people who are entitled to them since they meet eligibility criteria set by law
    B. federal program grants that state governments are entitled to receive only if the state laws and policies meet federal requirements
    C. federal programs that give special rights to a certain class of people or even animals, such as the Endangered Species Act
    D. federal programs that require women be given equal opportunities (such as in college sports programs) since they are entitled to equal treatment by law
    E. all government programs designed to ensure minorities get the equal protection of the law to which all citizens are entitled

33. Where in the federal court system do juries composed of ordinary citizens operate?

    A. in U.S. District Courts only
    B. in all federal courts except the Supreme Court
    C. in U.S. District Courts, U.S. Courts of Appeals, and, in unusual circumstances, the U.S. Supreme Court
    D. in U.S. District Courts and, only in cases involving criminal law, the U.S. Courts of Appeals
    E. nowhere—all cases in federal courts are decided by judges, not juries

34. The president generally plays the role of national leader rather than Congress for all of the following reasons EXCEPT

    A. The members of Congress are elected directly by the people, rather than by a group of electors like the president.
    B. The fragmented leadership of Congress makes it difficult for Congress to act quickly and decisively.
    C. The president gets most of the attention of the national media, making it easier for him to set the national agenda.

D. Congress is often stalemated, especially when different parties control the different houses of Congress.

E. The president as commander in chief and chief executive can issue orders to the military and the federal bureaucracy while Congress cannot.

35. Which of the following are results of the growth in the number of news outlets on the Internet and cable television?

I.   the rise of opinionated journalism

II. more in-depth coverage of national issues and problems by the news media

III. the decline of traditional newspapers and newsmagazines

IV. more competition among news sources for the audience share needed to generate advertising revenue and make a profit

A. statements I, II, and III only

B. statements I and III only

C. statements III and IV only

D. statements I, III, and IV only

E. statement III only

36. In the American system of government, state governments have the power to do all of the following EXCEPT

A. levy income taxes

B. make agreements with other states

C. regulate health care

D. establish their own court systems

E. regulate trade between their state and neighboring states

CONGRESSIONAL BILLS VETOED

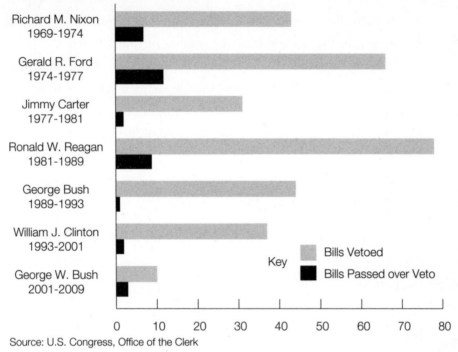

Source: U.S. Congress, Office of the Clerk

37. Which one of the following statements is best supported by the data in the bar graph above?

   A. Few bills are passed by Congress after being vetoed.

   B. The number of bills the president vetoes tends to vary depending on how long the president is in office.

   C. With the increasing political partisanship in Washington, presidential vetoes are becoming more frequent.

   D. Although Congress can easily override a president's veto, it seldom takes up a bill again after it has been vetoed.

   E. Since the Supreme Court's ruling in *Bush v. Gore* (2000), presidents have been advised by the Court to veto fewer bills.

38. What is the role of the National Security Council?

    A.   It identifies people who may be suspected terrorists.

    B.   It unifies the three different branches of the military.

    C.   It brings together the president, the leadership of Congress, the Department of Defense, and the Department of State to create the foreign policy of the United States.

    D.   It advises the president on all matters relating to national security.

    E.   It monitors the different intelligence agencies to ensure that they are working together.

39. Studies have shown that the most important influences on the development of a person's political values, beliefs, and identity are the person's

    A.   friends

    B.   parents

    C.   colleagues at work

    D.   religious leaders

    E.   teachers

40. The poll tax—a tax that had the effect of disenfranchising many African Americans in the South—was eliminated by

    A.   the Fourteenth Amendment (1868)

    B.   the Civil Rights Act of 1964

    C.   the Twenty-fourth Amendment (1964)

    D.   the Voting Rights Act of 1965

    E.   *Virginia v. Loving* (1967)

41. Which of the following is an example of devolution?

    A.   the Welfare Reform Act (1996), which gives more power to state governments in deciding how federal welfare funds will be administered

B.   the No Child Left Behind Act (2002), which sets federal stan-
     dards to define failing schools and specifies options to address
     the problem

C.   the Voting Rights Act (1965), which put state and local gov-
     ernments with histories of racial discrimination under federal
     supervision

D.   the Civil Rights Act (1964), which invalidated state and local
     laws requiring racial segregation

E.   the Americans with Disabilities Act (1990), which required
     state governments to make public buildings accessible to per-
     sons with disabilities

42. The specific regulations necessary to carry out most laws passed by
     Congress are written by

A.   congressional committees

B.   the federal courts as they interpret the law

C.   the Executive Office of the President, which writes all federal
     regulations under the authority of the president

D.   Department of Justice under the authority of the Attorney
     General

E.   the federal agency or agencies that will be enforcing the law

43. Pork-barrel spending involves

A.   funding popular entitlement programs likely to increase sup-
     port for senators' and representatives' reelection campaigns

B.   funding popular projects in senators' and representatives' home
     districts/states to help them get reelected

C.   funding agricultural subsidies for hog farmers

D.   funding federal programs to combat obesity and other national
     health problems

E.   deficit spending as a national economic policy in order to stim-
     ulate the economy

PERCENT OF VOTING-AGE POPULATION REPORTING THAT THEY VOTED

Characteristics	1980	1984	1988	1992	1996	2000	2004	2008
Total	59.2	59.9	57.4	61.3	54.2	54.7	58.3	58.2
18 to 20 years old	35.7	36.7	33.2	38.5	31.2	28.4	41.0	41.0
21 to 24 years old	43.1	43.5	38.3	45.7	33.4	35.4	42.5	46.6
25 to 34 years old	54.6	54.5	48.0	53.2	43.1	43.7	46.9	48.5
35 to 44 years old	64.4	63.5	61.3	63.6	54.9	55.0	56.9	55.2
45 to 64 years old	69.3	69.8	67.9	70.0	64.4	64.1	66.6	65.0
65 years old and over	65.1	67.7	68.8	70.1	67.0	67.6	68.9	68.1
Male	59.1	59.0	56.4	60.2	52.8	53.1	56.3	55.7
Female	59.4	60.8	58.3	62.3	55.5	56.2	60.1	60.4
School years completed:								
8 years or less	42.6	42.9	36.7	35.1	28.1	26.8	23.6	23.4
High school:								
Less than high school graduate	45.6	44.4	41.3	41.2	33.8	33.6	34.6	33.7
High school graduate or GED	58.9	58.7	54.7	57.5	49.1	49.4	52.4	50.9
College:								
Some college or associate's degree	67.2	67.5	64.5	68.7	60.5	60.3	66.1	65.0
Bachelor's or advanced degree	79.9	79.1	77.6	81.0	73.0	72.0	74.2	73.3

Source: U.S. Census Bureau

44. Which of the following statements is/are supported by the data shown in the table above?

I.   The more schooling a person has, the more likely it is that the person will vote.

II.   Men are more likely to vote than women.

III. Generally, the older a person is, the more likely it is that the person will vote.

IV.   In the 2004 and 2008 elections, young people were much more likely to vote than they had been in 1996 and 2000.

A. statements I, II, and III only

B. statements I and III only

C. statements III and IV only

D. statements I, III, and IV only

E. statements I, II, III, and IV

45. The legal action challenging one's imprisonment by appealing to a higher court to review the case is called

A. eminent domain

B. a writ of certiorari

C. a writ of habeas corpus

D. an amicus curie brief

E. a bill of attainder

46. The decisions of federal judges are based on all of the following EXCEPT

A. the wording of the Constitution

B. the intention of Congress when the actual wording of a federal law is ambiguous

C. the facts of the case as determined by the trial court

D. the wording of state laws

E. precedents established by decisions of the Supreme Court in related cases

47. The chief role of political parties in the American political system is to

A. get more people to vote

B. define the issues of an election through the party's platform

C. enact laws that carry out the party's platform if its candidates win election

D. elect its candidates to public office

E. conduct voter register drives to get more people registered

48. Interest groups frequently use all the following tactics to influence public policy EXCEPT

    A. providing federal agencies and Congress with information that supports the interest group's position
    B. raising campaign funds for a senator or representative that is a strong supporter of the interest group's position
    C. offering bribes to get members of Congress to support their position
    D. endorsing a candidate for public office and urging their members to support her/him
    E. getting members of the interest group to contact their senators and representatives to urge them to support the interest group's position

49. Which statement below best describes redistricting?

    A. the reallocation of seats in the House of Representatives to states based on their population after a new census
    B. the redrawing of electoral districts by Congress, usually in such a way as to protect the seats of incumbent congressmen
    C. the redrawing of electoral districts for U.S. senators based on the state's population after a new census
    D. redrawing the jurisdictional boundaries of federal district courts
    E. the redrawing of congressional districts by each state (usually by state legislature) after a new census

50. Under the principle of judicial review,

    A. the Supreme Court can review legislation under consideration by Congress and provide an opinion on its constitutionality
    B. state supreme courts can declare federal laws unconstitutional if they violate the state's constitution
    C. federal courts can declare federal and state laws unconstitutional
    D. judges must follow precedents established by previous Supreme Court decisions
    E. regulations proposed by a federal agency must be reviewed by a federal judge before going into effect

SELECTED CHARACTERISTICS OF MEMBERS OF CONGRESS

	Gender		Race	
	Male	Female	Black	Hispanic
REPRESENTATIVES				
94th Congress, 1975	416	19	17	7
96th Congress, 1979	417	16	17	5
98th Congress, 1983	413	21	21	8
100th Congress, 1987	412	23	23	11
102d Congress, 1991	407	28	26	11
104th Congress, 1995	388	47	40	17
106th Congress, 1999	379	56	39	19
108th Congress, 2003	376	59	39	22
110th Congress, 2007	361	74	42	23
SENATORS				
94th Congress, 1975	100	0	1	1
96th Congress, 1979	99	1	0	0
98th Congress, 1983	98	2	0	0
100th Congress, 1987	98	2	0	0
102d Congress, 1991	98	2	0	0
104th Congress, 1995	92	8	1	0
106th Congress, 1999	91	9	0	0
108th Congress, 2003	86	14	0	0
110th Congress, 2007	84	16	1	3

Source: U.S. Census Bureau from data published in Congressional Directory

51. Which of the following statements is NOT supported by the data in the table above?

A. Of the underrepresented groups shown in the table, women have made the most progress since 1975.

B. Congress remains predominantly white and male.

C. Of all underrepresented groups shown here, only women have developed a significant presence in the Senate.

D. The percentage of women in Congress will soon reflect the population breakdown of the United States.

E. In the 110th Congress, there were more African American members than members with Hispanic backgrounds.

52. The traditional view of the American political system as government by the majority would best be supported by

    A. election data showing that elections are usually won by the candidate spending the most money on his/her election campaign
    B. historical data showing that policy regarding petroleum production has been strongly influenced by interest groups representing petroleum companies
    C. studies that show day-to-day governmental decisions are made by unelected administrators based on their own views and interests
    D. a study of the Food and Drug Administration's decision-making regarding allowing new drugs on the market
    E. data showing that the votes of senators and representatives on legislation closely reflect public opinion polls in their districts or states

53. To manage the vast federal bureaucracy with its 2.5 million government workers, the president most relies on

    A. Congress
    B. the Office of Management and Budget (OMB)
    C. the General Accountability Office (GAO)
    D. the cabinet
    E. the vice president

54. Which of the following statements correctly describe/describes federalism today?

    I. State governments often adopt policies requested by the federal government in order to remain eligible for federal grants.
    II. State and federal governments often work together to jointly fund programs to deal with national problems.
    III. A well-defined line separates policy areas controlled by the federal government and policy areas controlled by state governments.

IV. The role of the national government is growing in most areas of public policy, including areas that have traditionally been reserved for the states.

A. statements I, III, and IV only

B. statements I, II, and IV only

C. statements I and II only

D. statements II and IV only

E. statement I, II, III, and IV

55. The due-process clause of the Fourteenth Amendment has been interpreted by the Supreme Court to

A. protect the rights of the accused in criminal proceedings

B. protect people from unreasonable searches and seizures

C. require government to provide the "equal protection of the law" to all citizens

D. limit the government's power to take private property for public use

E. extend the protections of the Bill of Rights to the actions of state governments

56. Which of the following powers can the president exercise without getting explicit approval from Congress?

A. his power to command the armed forces

B. his power to appoint ambassadors

C. his power to enter into treaties with other nations

D. his power to name the secretary of state

E. his power to appoint U.S. representatives to international organizations

57. What is the role of the appropriations committees in Congress?

   A. They set the rules for floor debate on a bill, appropriating time to each side for their speeches.

   B. They authorize federal programs, determining which are appropriate and which are not.

   C. They consider taxation bills.

   D. They consider all bills that provide funding for the federal government.

   E. They must approve the federal regulations written by federal agencies.

58. Which of the following is a result of the Electoral College system?

   A. the focus on undecided voters

   B. the focus on the small states since they are disproportionately represented in the Electoral College

   C. the focus only on a few states where polls show the vote is very close

   D. the focus on fundraising

   E. the focus on "swing" electors who may be undecided

59. Which of the following officials CANNOT be removed from office through actions taken by another branch of the government?

   A. the president

   B. justices of the Supreme Court

   C. federal judges in courts below the Supreme Court

   D. U.S. senators and representatives

   E. the secretaries that head the federal government departments

60. Political parties engage in all of the following activities EXCEPT

    A.   organizing a party leadership structure at local, state, and national levels

    B.   conducting voter registration drives in communities likely to be supportive of the party

    C.   raising money for the party's candidates

    D.   withholding funds and support from party candidates who don't support the positions of the party as expressed in the party platform

    E.   organizing national conventions to select the party's candidates for president and vice president

Section II
Time—100 minutes
Four Questions

Directions: You have 100 minutes to answer the following four questions. Unless the directions indicate otherwise, respond to all parts of all four questions. Spend approximately one-fourth of your time (25 minutes) on each question. In your response, use substantive examples where appropriate. Make certain to number each of your answers as the question is numbered below.

1. The concept of federalism has changed as the relationship between national and state governments has evolved.

    (a) Explain the roles of state and national governments under the doctrine of dual federalism.

    (b) Today the concept of dual federalism is largely outdated and the concepts of fiscal federalism and cooperative federalism have replaced it. Describe both fiscal federalism and cooperative federalism as they apply to the relationship between state and national governments today. Use appropriate examples.

    (c) Below are listed three clauses of the Constitution. For each of these three clauses, describe the clause, how it has been interpreted by the Supreme Court, and how this interpretation has increased the power of the federal government relative to state governments.

    • Supremacy clause

    • Interstate commerce clause

    • Due-process clause of the Fourteenth Amendment

2. The vast federal bureaucracy, consisting of 2.5 million workers, is widely regarded as slow to respond and hard to control.

   (a) The president, as head of the executive branch, is the chief executive officer of the federal bureaucracy. Explain two reasons why it is difficult for the president to control the federal bureaucracy.

   (b) Describe three powers the president has that he can use to control the bureaucracy. For each power, give an example of how it can be used to control the bureaucracy.

   (c) Describe two powers Congress has to control the bureaucracy. For each power, give an example of how it can be used to control the bureaucracy.

3. Political parties and interest groups play an important role in the American political system.

   (a) Describe two activities that both political parties and interest groups engage in.

   (b) Describe two activities that political parties engage in that interest groups do not.

   (c) Describe two activities that interest groups engage in that political parties do not.

PRESIDENTIAL VOTE IN YEARS WITH STRONG THIRD PARTY CANDIDATE

Year	Candidate	Party	Popular Vote	Electoral Vote
1948	Truman	Democratic	49.4%	57.1%
	Dewey	Republican	45.0%	35.6%
	Thurmond	States' Rights	2.4%	7.3%
1968	Nixon	Republican	43.4%	35.5%
	Humphrey	Democratic	42.4%	55.9%
	Wallace	American Independent	12.9%	8.6%
1980	Reagan	Republican	50.5%	90.9%
	Carter	Democratic	41.0%	9.1%
	Anderson	Independent (no party)	6.1%	0.0%
1992	Clinton	Democratic	42.9%	68.8%
	George H.W. Bush	Republican	37.1%	31.2%
	Perot	Independent (no party)	18.9%	0.0%

Source: U.S. House of Representatives, Office of the Clerk

4. Third parties—parties other than the two dominant political parties—rarely play an important role in the American political system. Refer to the table above to help answer the questions below.

    (a) Explain why the percentages of the popular vote won by presidential candidates are seldom even close to the percentages of the electoral vote won by the candidates.

    (b) Explain why third party candidates in 1948 and 1968 got electoral votes but in 1980 and 1992 third party candidates did not.

    (c) Describe a scenario in which a third party could prevent the Electoral College from selecting the president. How would the president be selected in that case?

    (d) Explain a scenario in which a third party could determine the outcome of a presidential election even if it gets no electoral votes.

    (e) Explain why it is likely that a sizable number of voters in the elections shown in the table actually liked a third party candidate better but voted for one of the two major-party candidates instead.

Answer Key, Section I

1.E	21. E	41. A
2.B	22. E	42. E
3.C	23. B	43. B
4.B	24. E	44. D
5.A	25. B	45. C
6.A	26. E	46. D
7.C	27. A	47. D
8.D	28. D	48. C
9.C	29. C	49. E
10. D	30. C	50. C
11. C	31. D	51. D
12. B	32. A	52. E
13. A	33. A	53. B
14. A	34. A	54. B
15. E	35. D	55. E
16. E	36. E	56. A
17. A	37. A	57. D
18. D	38. D	58. C
19. C	39. B	59. D
20. A	40. C	60. D

Section I Answers and Explanations

1. E. Congress must approve any expenditure of government funds. The president submits his budget request and Congress take whatever action it sees fit, often checking the power of the president, either by rejecting funds the president wants or specifying funds that must be spent in a way the president opposes. It takes a two-thirds majority to override a veto (answer choice A). The Supreme Court cannot review executive orders until a case works its way through the court system, often years later (answer choice B). In regard to answer choice C, only the Senate can reject or ratify a treaty; the House gets no say. Since the president nominates judges, it is impossible for the Senate to select a judge the president doesn't support (answer choice D).

2. B. The Tenth Amendment reserves powers for the states and is thus not a reason for the federal government's dominance over state governments. All the other answer choices are factors that have contributed to the supremacy of the federal government over state governments.

3. C. Pluralism refers to the political process in which multiple interest groups compete with each other to determine public policy. Some argue that this process, usually involving compromise, produces good government, but others point out that the process gives well-funded interest groups (especially those representing big corporations) an unfair advantage. None of the other answer choices describe pluralism.

4. B. When the House and Senate pass different versions of legislation, a conference committee consisting of senators and representatives is formed to negotiate a compromise. The compromise approved by the conference committee must then be passed by both houses of Congress in order to go to the president for his signature and become law. Standing committees (answer choice A) in the House and Senate dominate the legislative process, but the conference committee is a temporary committee, not a standing committee, although it is composed of key members of the standing committees

in both houses. The process of negotiating a compromise between the House and Senate versions of the legislation is known as "reconciliation" but there is no such thing as a "reconciliation committee" in Congress (answer choice C).

5. A. Women, African Americans, and union households all are significantly more likely to support the Democratic candidate than men, whites, and nonunion households. Thus, statements I, II, and III are correct. In regard to statement IV, people with a college or advanced degree break down about evenly between Democratic and Republican candidates, making this statement incorrect.

6. A. The delegates at the Constitutional Convention wanted to insulate judges from political pressure, thus they provided life terms for judges so they would not need to worry about getting reelected or reappointed. Judges can be impeached by Congress; however, this has happened only in extremely rare cases. None of the other answer choices describe goals the delegates considered when specifying life terms for judges.

7. C. The term "open seats" is used to describe elections for seats in Congress in which there is no incumbent running. Obviously, if senators are limited to only two terms, there would be more open seats since now senators are often elected for more than two terms. None of the other answer choices could be expected to change as a result of term limits for senators. The committee system (answer choice A) would still function (albeit with greater turnover of committee members) and senators could still be elected to a second term as before (answer choice D). The vice president would still serve as President of the Senate (answer choice B) and there is no reason to believe that having more open seats would lead to more African Americans being elected (answer choice E).

8. D. In *Texas v. Johnson* the Supreme Court held that flag-burning, as a means of protest, was symbolic free speech protected by the First Amendment. In regard to answer choice A, *Griswold v. Connecticut*

involved the right to privacy, which is not a First Amendment right, but a right implied by the Bill of Rights as a whole. Gun ownership (answer choice C) is addressed in the Second Amendment and the rights of the accused (answer choices B and E) are addressed in the Fifth and Sixth Amendments.

9. C. Three-fourths of the states must approve any constitutional amendment. The president cannot formally submit an amendment or veto one (answer choices A and E); in fact, the president is not officially involved in the process of amending the Constitution. Congress must approve a proposed amendment by a two-thirds majority in both houses (answer choice D) in order to submit it to the states for ratification. The people of the United States have no direct say in the process of amending the Constitution (answer choice B), although they can try to influence their elected representatives in Congress and their state legislature.

10. D. The party base that votes in a primary election is not representative of the electorate as a whole. The Democratic Party base is to the left of center and the Republican Party base is to the right. Both Democratic and Republican candidates usually try to move to the center of the political spectrum after winning the primary to improve their chances of winning the election. In regard to answer choice B, fundraising is more successful with appeals to the party base, rather than the middle, where more uncommitted voters reside.

11. C. It's all or nothing—the president must veto the entire bill or not veto it at all. All of the other answer choices correctly describe options open to the president when a bill is passed by Congress.

12. B. The Court's decision in *Brown v. Board of Education* established that segregated schools could never provide the "equal protection of the law" that the Fourteenth Amendment requires states to give all of their citizens. In regard to answer choice A, only seventeen years later when faced with the persistence of segregated schools, did the court move to require busing to achieve racial balance (*Swann v.*

Charlotte-Mecklenburg County Board of Education, 1971). *Brown v. Board of Education* overturned *Plessy v. Ferguson* (1896), which ruled that segregated schools did not violate the Fourteenth Amendment (answer choice C). The position described in answer choice D is one the Supreme Court has never taken. Strict quota systems (answer choice E) were declared unconstitutional in *University of California Regents v. Bakke* (1978).

13. A. The standing committees dominate the legislative process in the area of their jurisdiction and the chair of each standing committee has considerable power in determining whether a bill gets considered, what the content of the bill is, and whether or not it passes. Answer choice B is incorrect because the vice president, although officially serving as President of the Senate, actually has very little power in the Senate except to break tie votes. The majority leader in the Senate leads the Senate but in the House it is the Speaker of the House, not the majority leader, that leads the majority party (answer choice C). Seniority and expertise are helpful (answer choices D and E), but not the deciding factors in determining power. Typically, the chairs of the standing committees have both seniority and expertise in the area of their committee's jurisdiction, but it is their position as chair that gives them power.

14. A. The news media play an important role in our political system that includes answer choices B through E. However, the broadcast news media, due to the equal-time rule established by the Federal Communications Commission, must provide equal treatment to all candidates for a political office. If a television or radio station/network accepts the paid political advertising of one candidate, it must also do so for the candidate's opponents. The equal-time rule further requires that if a television or radio station provides free airtime for one candidate (in an interview on a news program, for example), it must also offer the same to the other candidates.

15. E. A country's political culture includes the underlying core values and beliefs shared by virtually all its citizens. Answer choices A through D are all core values/beliefs shared by virtually all Americans on the left and right. However, the belief that government has gotten too big is a controversial issue on which Americans do not share the same opinion.

16. E. After adjusting for inflation, the increase in 2009 was 23.3 percent—a much greater increase than any other year shown in the table. Constant dollars show values adjusted for inflation; three years show a decrease in federal grants in constant dollars, making answer choice A incorrect. The increase between 2000 and 2009 in current dollars was about 280 *billion*, making answer choice B incorrect. In regard to answer choice C, between 2000 and 2009, federal grants to state and local governments only doubled before adjusting for inflation. In regard to answer choice D, grants before adjusting for inflation increased by 5 percent in 2005; 0.9 percent is the increase after adjusting for inflation.

17. A. This answer choice states the trend shown in the table. Answer choice B is incorrect because there is a clear long-term trend, even if 2009 is excluded as an aberration. In regard to answer choice C, the table makes no judgment on how to best measure the increase in grants—current or constant dollars—it just presents the facts measured in two different ways. However, adjusting for inflation probably gives the best picture of reality since the value of the dollar in current dollars changes. In regard to answer choice D, the table makes no judgment regarding what should be done; it just presents facts. Answer choice E is incorrect because just because grants have increased in the past is no reason to conclude that this will continue forever—we need more information before trying to predict the future.

18. D. The Warren Court (1953–1969) is a classic example of judicial activism. It especially pursued an activist role in civil rights and protection of the rights of the accused. Judicial restraint (answer choice

C) is the opposite of judicial activism. Judicial review (answer choice E), the doctrine that the Supreme Court can declare laws unconstitutional, was established in *Marbury v. Madison* (1803) and is not specifically associated with the Warren Court. Throughout the twentieth century the Supreme Court did not hesitate to use its power of judicial review to declare laws unconstitutional. The doctrine of original intent (answer choice B) was not important to the Warren Court nor did the Warren Court invoke dual federalism—the idea that state and federal governments are each sovereign in their own areas of policy (answer choice A). Instead, it supported federal government involvement in areas state governments traditionally controlled.

19. C. Other than succeeding the president if he dies, the vice president's sole constitutional role is to preside over the Senate—a role with little actual power except the power to break tie votes. Vice presidents do not play a leadership role in Congress (answer choice A) nor do they head the cabinet (answer choice B). Vice presidents may represent the United States overseas (answer choice D) or serve as a liaison between the president and Congress (answer choice E) if the president delegates this role, but these are not roles given the vice president by the Constitution.

20. A. After committee hearings, the committee generally debates the bill, amends it, and votes. In regard to answer choice B, subcommittees are never formed *after* hearings are conducted; subcommittees in the House and Senate are usually standing subcommittees that often hold the hearings on behalf of the full committee. The Rules Committee (answer choice C) only exists in the House and it only gets involved after the full committee has voted on the bill and reported it to the full House for floor debate. The Supreme Court (answer choice D) does not get involved until a law is passed and challenged in court, a process that can take a couple of years. The bill does not go to the other house of Congress until the house where it was introduced passes the bill (answer choice E).

21. E is the correct answer choice. Each state makes its own laws governing federal elections within its boundaries. Of course, these laws must be consistent with the U.S. Constitution, including the amendments granting African Americans, women, and eighteen-year-olds the right to vote. The Federal Election Commission (answer choice A) is mainly concerned with enforcing campaign finance laws and does not regulate the election itself. Congress (answer choice B) has only limited power to enact election laws, but through the incentive of federal grants has encouraged states to adopt certain measures relating to elections such as the "Motor Voter Law." The Attorney General and Department of Justice generally do not get involved; the exception is that under the Voting Rights Law of 1965, the Justice Department can review voting procedures in states and counties with a history of discrimination to make sure there is no ongoing racial discrimination.

22. E. States retained most of the power and the national government lacked the power to do much of anything without getting the consent of the states. Answer choice A is incorrect because George Washington was the first president under the U.S. Constitution but not directly involved in the national government under the Articles of Confederation, except to serve as general during the War of Independence. There was no Supreme Court under the Articles of Confederation (answer choice B). Answer choice C is incorrect, because, while there was only a legislative branch under the Articles, it was not dominated by the larger states—each state got one vote. In regard to answer choice D, there was no judicial branch under the Articles of Confederation, but there was a legislative branch, known as the Continental Congress.

23. B is the correct answer choice. The Supreme Court agrees to consider a case if four of the nine justices vote to hear the case. The Chief Justice (answer choice A) has no power to set the Court's agenda; he is just considered "the first among equals." The U.S. Courts of Appeals (answer choice E) are not involved in deciding what cases

should go to the Supreme Court. The Attorney General is also generally not involved (answer choice D), but the Department of Justice sometimes requests that the Court hear a case involving the U.S. government as one of the parties, and the Court usually complies.

24. E. The table doesn't show how people voted (or if they voted), only which party they identified with or leaned toward. In fact, in four of the six years shown in the table, Republican presidents were elected in spite of the Democratic edge in party identification. All the other statements are supported by data in the table.

25. B. Political socialization is the process through which individuals acquire their political beliefs, values, and identity. All the other answer choices are incorrect because they contradict the correct answer.

26. E. The War Powers Resolution, originally passed in 1973 over Nixon's veto, was intended to limit the power of the president to engage U.S. troops in combat abroad without the approval of Congress. Congress saw it as a way of preserving a check on the president's power to wage war, since in the second half of the twentieth century, actual declarations of war (a power of Congress) became outmoded. The president, as commander in chief, engaged U.S. troops in wars in Korea, Vietnam, Iraq, Afghanistan, etc., without congressional declarations of war. None of the other answer choices are related to the War Powers Resolution.

27. A. If no candidate gets a majority of the electoral vote (the vote is tied or there are more than two candidates getting electoral votes), then the House of Representatives chooses the president from the top three vote-getters in the electoral vote. For this purpose, each state, regardless of the number of representatives, gets one vote. If no candidate for vice president gets a majority of the electoral vote, then the Senate chooses the vice president (answer choice B). To select the president, there is no second ballot in the Electoral College (answer choice D), and no joint session of Congress (answer choice C). The Supreme Court (answer choice E) is not involved except

to rule on disputes regarding procedures, as happened in 2000 with *Bush v. Gore*.

28. D. In *Engle v. Vitale*, the Supreme Court held that the recitation of a prayer written by the school board in the public schools violated the establishment clause of the First Amendment, which states "Government shall make no law respecting an establishment of religion..." Individuals remained free to exercise their religion, including praying if they wanted to, so the decision did not involve the free-exercise clause of the First Amendment (answer choice D). The Fifth Amendment right to remain silent relates to persons accused of a crime and was not relevant to the issue in *Engle v. Vitale* (answer choice B). The freedom of speech (answer choice A) was also not relevant to the case since individual students remained free to speak out for or against school prayer or to pray if they wanted to. The right to privacy was also not an issue; in fact it was not recognized by the Supreme Court until *Griswold v. Connecticut* in 1965.

29. C. The Great Compromise produced a Congress consisting of two houses. In the Senate each state gets equal representation while in the House of Representatives, each state gets representation based on its population. Federalism (answer choice A) was not a compromise; the goal of maintaining independent state governments while strengthening the federal government was shared by all the delegates to the Constitutional Convention, although there was disagreement on exactly how much power the federal government should have. Answer choice B is incorrect because small states do not get equal representation in Congress—only in the Senate. Answer choice D is incorrect because no delegates suggested senators should be elected by the people. In fact, until the Seventeenth Amendment was passed in 1913, senators were elected by state legislatures. Answer choice E describes a compromise that was made at the Constitutional Convention, but this is known as the Three-Fifths Compromise.

30. C. Single-member congressional districts and the winner-take-all system in the Electoral College mean that it is very difficult for third parties to gain enough power to play any role in government. Answer choice A is obviously false and the Constitution makes no mention of political parties (answer choice D). Polls show that many Americans are not often happy with the choices offered by the two dominant political parties (answer choice B) and more people actually identify themselves as independents than as Republicans or Democrats (answer choice E).

31. D. More people go to the polls in years in which the president is being elected than in the midterm elections. This means that more people vote for their U.S. representative every four years when they are also voting for president. Answer choice A is incorrect because all members of the House of Representatives have two-year terms and are elected in both midterm and presidential elections. Answer choice B is incorrect because more people vote in presidential election years than in midterm elections. Answer choice C is a correct statement, but this information is not shown in the graph. The drop-off in voter turnout in midterm elections is highly predictable and consistent, making answer choice E incorrect.

32. A. Entitlement programs are programs that provide benefits to people who are entitled to the benefits since they meet the criteria set in the law. Social Security, Medicare, and veterans benefits are examples of entitlement programs. The other answer choices contradict the correct answer choice and are incorrect.

33. A. Juries of ordinary citizens can be found in many cases in U.S. District Courts. These are the courts of original jurisdiction in the federal system, so this is where trials are held. Appeals courts review the record of the trial to see that the law was properly interpreted and followed, but do not conduct a new trial. In rare cases (such as a dispute between state governments) the Supreme Court is also a court of original jurisdiction and conducts a trial, but in these cases,

the "jury" is the nine justices of the Court, not a jury of ordinary citizens. Thus all the other answer choices are incorrect.

34. A. The fact that the president is elected by the Electoral College and members of Congress directly by the people does not affect either's abilities to provide national leadership. The delegates at the Constitutional Convention envisioned that Congress would perform the leadership role in American government. They gave most of the power of the federal government to Congress, including the powers to declare war, pass laws, determine the federal budget, and approve the appointment of judges and officials. All the answer choices except A help to explain why the president has assumed the role of national leadership in the modern world rather than Congress.

35. D. The rise of multiple news outlets on the Internet and cable television has led to a rise in opinionated journalism, the decline of traditional newspapers and newsmagazines, and a more competitive business environment for news programs/sources. However, the increase in competition has not led to more in-depth coverage of national issues and problems, since this type of programming tends to be more expensive to produce and is less likely to generate a large audience.

36. E. The Constitution gives the federal government the power to control interstate commerce. The Supreme Court has further ruled that the power to regulate and control interstate commerce lies exclusively with the federal government and states cannot interfere in this area (*Gibbons v. Ogden*, 1824). All of the other answer choices list powers of state governments. Virtually all states tax incomes and all states make agreements with other states, have their own court systems, and regulate health care (for example, setting the requirements for licensing of doctors and nurses and operating hospitals and nursing homes).

37. A. Only a small percentage of bills vetoed by the president are passed by Congress over the president's veto. The number of bills a

president vetoes is not closely related to how long the president is in office (answer choice B). For example, Ford spent only two years in office but vetoed 66 bills. Despite increasing partisanship, the number of bills vetoed is not growing (answer choice C). Congress is actually required by the Constitution to reconsider a bill after the president's veto (answer choice D). In regard to answer choice E, Bush v. Gore had nothing to do with the president's veto power and the Supreme Court never serves as an adviser to the president.

38. D. The National Security Council (NSC) advises the president on national security matters. The NSC is chaired by the president and includes the vice president, Secretary of State, Secretary of Defense, Chairman of the Joint Chiefs of Staff, Director of National Intelligence, and members of the president's staff. None of the other answer choices describe something the National Security Council does.

39. B. Parents are the most important influence on the political socialization process through which a person acquires his/her political values, beliefs, and identity. The persons listed in the other answer choices also influence the political socialization process, but they are not as important as parents.

40. C. The poll tax was eliminated in 1964 with the ratification of the Twenty-fourth Amendment.

41. A. Devolution is the delegation of more power to state governments in administering federal programs and grants. The Welfare Reform Act, which gave state and local governments more power over how federal welfare funds are spent, is a classic example of devolution. All of the other answer choices list laws that *increased* the power of the federal government in areas traditionally under state control.

42. E. After a law is passed, the specific regulations needed to enforce the law are generally written by the federal agency that will be enforcing the law. Congress and the federal courts (answer choices A and B) are not involved in the writing of these regulations. The president and Department of Justice (answer choices C and D) are usually not

directly involved in the writing of regulations, although the president can intervene or ask the Justice Department to intervene if he wishes. Federal regulations are considered administrative law and have the full force of law that laws written by Congress (statutory law) have.

43. B. Pork-barrel spending refers to the funding of popular projects in the home district/state of senators and representatives to help them get reelected. Funding popular entitlement programs (answer choice A) could also help members of Congress get reelected, but this doesn't specifically help the member of Congress's home district/state more than others and is not referred to as pork-barrel spending. Similarly, federal health programs (answer choice D) and agricultural subsidies (answer choice C) are not generally considered pork-barrel spending since they don't usually bring a special benefit to a particular congressional district or state. Although pork-barrel spending (which doesn't always involve deficit spending) may have an effect in stimulating the national economy, the purpose of pork-barrel spending is to bring federal projects to a district/state, not to create national economic policy (answer choice E).

44. D. The data in the table support statements I, III, and IV. The data also show that since 1980 women have been more likely to vote than men, making Statement II incorrect.

45. C. A writ of habeas corpus refers to the legal action of challenging a person's imprisonment by appealing to a court of law. Eminent domain (answer choice A) refers to the power of government to take private property for public use. A writ of certiorari (answer choice B) refers to a legal action requiring a lower court to turn over the records of a trial so that the case can be reviewed by a higher court. An amicus curiae brief (answer choice D) is a legal argument on a case before a court that is submitted by a party (called a "friend of the court") that has a stake in the outcome of the case but is not one of the parties directly involved. A bill of attainder (answer choice E) is a legislative act declaring a person (or group of persons) guilty of

a crime and imposing a punishment without holding a trial; bills of attainder are prohibited by the U.S. Constitution.

46. D. Federal judges do not interpret or enforce state laws; this is the role of state courts. The wording of state laws is of no importance to federal judges, unless the case involves determining whether or not a state law violates federal law or the Constitution, in which case, the federal judge's decision is based on federal law or the Constitution. The decisions of federal judges are based on the Constitution (answer choice A), federal laws, the intent of Congress if the actual wording is unclear (answer choice B), precedents (answer choice E), and the facts of the case as determined by the trial court (answer choice D).

47. D. The objective of political parties is to get their candidates elected. They don't care about getting more people to vote (answer choice A)—only about getting more of the supporters to vote so they can achieve their goal of getting their candidates elected. Similarly, they don't care about getting everyone registered to vote (answer choice E)—only about getting their likely supporters to register so they can improve their chances of getting their candidates elected. In regard to answer choice B, the candidates themselves define the issues and the party platform is of little importance; sometimes it's not even supported by the party's candidates. Once elected, the enactment of laws is left to elected representatives, not the party officials or party organization (answer choice C), which already becomes focused on winning the next election rather than governing.

48. C. Interest groups frequently engage in all the activities listed except bribery, which is illegal, and in the long run, usually hurts the interest group's public image. Of course, raising campaign funds for a senator or representative (answer choice B) is not that different, but this activity is legal. It is also different in that the money must be accounted for both in terms of where it comes from and how it is spent; it cannot be used for the personal gain of the candidate.

49. E. Redistricting is the redrawing of congressional districts by each state after a new census every ten years. The reallocation of seats in the House of Representatives (answer choice A) based on the new census is called reapportionment. Reapportionment by the federal government based on the new census must happen before the states can begin the redistricting process. Statement B is incorrect because state governments, not Congress, are responsible for redistricting. Statement C is incorrect because the election districts for senators are never redrawn—they are based on state boundaries and do not change. Reapportionment and redistricting apply only to the House of Representatives, where the number of representatives a state gets is based on population. Regarding answer choice D, the term "redistricting" is used to refer to Congress, not to changes in the boundaries of the jurisdiction of federal courts.

50. C. Judicial review refers to the power of courts to review laws and declare them unconstitutional, thus invalidating them. Federal courts can declare federal and state laws unconstitutional if they violate the U.S. Constitution. In regard to answer choice A, the Supreme Court cannot review legislation until it becomes law and is challenged in a lawsuit that makes its way through the federal court system. Regarding answer choice B, state courts can declare state laws unconstitutional if they violate the state's constitution, but state courts cannot declare federal laws unconstitutional if they violate the state's constitution because federal laws have supremacy over state constitutions. Judges are supposed to follow precedents (answer choice D), but the legal term for this is stare decisis, not judicial review. Federal judges don't review federal regulations until they are adopted and then challenged in a lawsuit (answer choice E).

51. D. There is no evidence in the table to indicate that the percentage of women in Congress will soon reflect the composition of the population. Although the percentage of women in Congress has been growing, this does not necessarily mean it will continue to grow—we need more information to make predictions regarding

future elections. Furthermore, women remain a long way from the 50 percent mark, so it appears unlikely that they will reach this benchmark anytime soon, even if the rate of increase is projected into the future. All of the other statements are supported by data in the table. In regard to answer choice B, there is no column listing the number of white members of Congress, but you should know there are 100 members of the Senate and 435 members of the House, so racial minorities still comprise only a small percentage of Congress, which remains predominantly white and male. In regard to answer choice E, you must add numbers of African Americans and people of Hispanic descent in both houses to determine which had the most members of Congress: There were 43 African Americans and 26 of Hispanic descent.

52. E. A study showing that the voting patterns of members of Congress follow public opinion in their districts would support the traditional idea of the government by the people through their elected representatives. Data showing that elections are usually won by the candidate spending the most money (answer choice A) would tend to support the view that a wealthy elite has more power in government than the people as a whole. Historical data showing the power of petroleum companies in making petroleum policy (answer choice B) would support the idea of wealthy interest groups dominating governmental decision-making, rather than the people as a whole. Studies that show that governmental power is wielded by unelected administrators based on their own views and interests (answer choice C) would not support the traditional view of government by the majority. A study of the Food and Drug Administration's decision-making (answer choice D) would not be a good example of government by the people; it would be likely to support theories of public policy created by powerful interest groups (such as the pharmaceutical companies) or public policy created by a an elite group (research scientists).

53. B. The president mostly relies on the OMB to control the bureaucracy. The OMB is part of the Executive Office of the President and

its powerful director reports directly to the president. The OMB supervises the budgetary process, controls the expenditure of money in the executive branch, and approves or rejects federal regulations that have budgetary implications. Due to its power to control the federal budget, Congress (answer choice A) does have considerable influence over the bureaucracy, but Congress is a legislative body, not an executive agency helping the president manage the bureaucracy. The GAO (answer choice C) is an agency reporting to Congress, not the president. It assists Congress in its oversight role, but does not manage the budget or the bureaucracy. The cabinet (answer choice D) is purely an advisory body. Finally, the vice president (answer choice E) has no constitutional role in the administration of the executive branch. Recent presidents have delegated authority to vice presidents to carry out certain tasks in the executive branch. Presidents, however, generally like to keep control of the federal bureaucracy as much as possible in their own hands.

54. B. Statements I, II, and IV correctly describe the operation of federalism today. Statement III is incorrect because today there is no well-defined line separating policy areas controlled by the federal government and policy areas controlled by the states. This traditional idea of separate policy areas with the federal and state governments, each sovereign in their own areas of policy, is called dual federalism. However, the federal government is now involved to some degree in all policy areas, often working with the states through jointly funded and administered programs.

55. E. In *Gitlow v. New York* (1925) the Supreme Court held that the due-process clause of the Fourteenth Amendment required state governments to act in accordance with the Bill of Rights, which was originally written to apply only to the federal government. The Fourteenth Amendment also requires state governments to provide the "equal protection of the law" to all its citizens (answer choice C), but this is known as the equal-protection clause. The Fifth Amendment guarantees the right to due process of law to persons

accused of a crime (answer choice A). The Fourth Amendment protects people from unreasonable searches and seizures (answer choice B). In regard to answer choice D, the Fifth Amendment limits the government's power to take private property (eminent domain) by requiring the due process of law and just compensation for the property owner.

56. A. The president is commander in chief of the U.S. military and does not need congressional approval to issue commands to the military. However, in regard to answer choices B, D, and E, the president does need the approval of the Senate in order to appoint ambassadors, representatives to international organizations (also considered ambassadors), and the Secretary of State. The president can negotiate a treaty (answer choice C), but in order for it to take effect (ratification), the Senate must approve the treaty by a two-thirds majority.

57. D. The appropriations committees are standing committees of the House and the Senate that consider all bills that provide funding for the federal government. In regard to answer choice A, the House Rules Committee sets the rules for floor debate on a bill; however, in the Senate there is no similar committee and floor debate is less restricted. The appropriations committees do not authorize programs (answer choice B); this is done by each of the other standing committees in their area of jurisdiction. The appropriations committees can only fund federal agencies and programs if they have been "authorized" by separate legislation. The appropriations committees do not consider taxation bills (answer choice C); this is done by the Ways and Means Committee in the House and the Finance Committee in the Senate. Neither Congress nor its committees approve federal regulations written by federal agencies (answer choice E).

58. C. Because of the winner-take-all system in the Electoral College, presidential candidates need to focus on those states where polls indicate the election is close. Winning more people's votes in a state

the candidate is already carrying does the candidate no good. Similarly, winning more votes in a state the candidate will lose anyway also is of no benefit to the candidate. Thus candidates campaign almost exclusively in "swing" states that could swing either way. In regard to answer choice A, presidential campaigns would be geared to undecided voters whether or not there is an Electoral College; the focus on undecided voters is not a result of the Electoral College system. Presidential candidates generally give little attention to small states (answer choice B), focusing mostly on the large swing states with the most electoral votes. Presidential candidates spend much of their time and effort on fundraising for their campaign, since running a campaign has become very expensive, especially producing television ads and airing them (answer choice D). However, this is not a result of the Electoral College system. In regard to answer choice E, there are no "swing" electors; all presidential electors are committed to a specific candidate. If a candidate wins the popular vote in a state, the electors that he has selected get to cast the state's electoral votes.

59. D. U.S. senators and representatives cannot be removed from office by another branch of government, although they can be expelled by a vote of the Senate or House itself. The Constitution gives both houses the power to expel their own members, but this has only happened on rare occasions. Usually members of Congress who violate ethics rules are punished in other ways—a fine, censure, or being forced to give up a committee chair—and members who commit a serious crime usually resign. Congress can impeach and remove from office officials of the other branches of government, including the president (answer choice A), the justices of the Supreme Court (answer choice B), lower federal judges (answer choice C), and the secretaries that head the federal departments (answer choice E) as well as ambassadors and other federal officials.

60. D. In the American political system, a party's candidates do not have to support the official positions of the party as expressed in the party

platform. In fact, they often don't. Especially now that the party's candidates are usually selected by primary elections, party officials have little control over the positions the candidate takes. All of the other answer choices describe the activities of political parties.

About the Author

Del Franz is a former teacher of social studies, including U.S. Government and Politics, at North Salem High School in Salem, Oregon. For the past seventeen years, he has worked in the field of test prep, producing books to help students score their best on standardized tests. He has developed test prep programs for two test-prep companies, including Kaplan. Franz also enjoys traveling the world, and has visited sixty-six countries. He currently lives in New Jersey, at the site of George Washington's crossing of the Delaware, with his partner and their five-year-old daughter.

Also Available

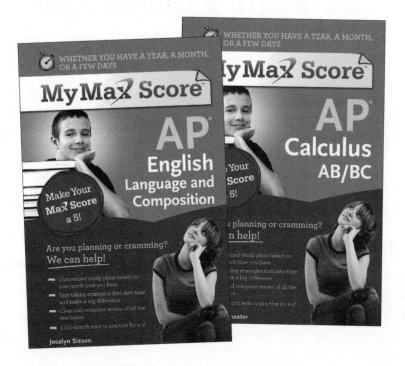

My Max Score AP U.S. History
by Michael Romano • 978-1-4022-4310-3

My Max Score AP English Literature and Composition
by Tony Armstrong • 978-1-4022-4311-0

My Max Score AP English Language and Composition
by Jocelyn Sisson • 978-1-4022-4312-7

My Max Score AP Calculus AB/BC
by Carolyn Wheater • 978-1-4022-4313-4

$14.99 U.S./ $17.99 CAN/ £9.99 UK

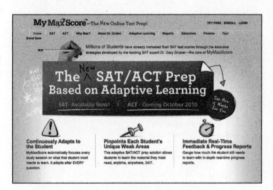

Essentials from
Dr. Gary Gruber
and the creators of My Max Score

"Gruber can ring the bell on any number
of standardized exams."
—*Chicago Tribune*

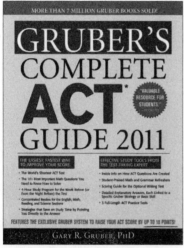

$19.99 U.S./ $23.99 CAN/ £14.99
978-1-4022-4307-3

$19.99 U.S./ $23.99 CAN/ £10.99
978-1-4022-3777-5

$16.99 U.S./ $19.99 CAN/ £11.99
978-1-4022-4308-0

$13.99 U.S./ $16.99 CAN/ £7.99
978-1-4022-3859-8

"Gruber's methods make the questions
seem amazingly simple to solve."
—*Library Journal*

"Gary Gruber is the leading expert on the SAT."
—*Houston Chronicle*

$14.99 U.S./ $15.99 CAN/ £7.99
978-1-4022-1846-0

$14.99 U.S./ $15.99 CAN/ £7.99
978-1-4022-1847-7

$14.99 U.S./ $15.99 CAN/ £7.99
978-1-4022-1848-4

$12.99 U.S./ $15.99 CAN/ £6.99
978-1-4022-2010-4